AIR CAMPAIGN

STALINGRAD AIRLIFT 1942–43

The Luftwaffe's broken promise to Sixth Army

T0322639

WILLIAM E. HIESTAND | ILLUSTRATED BY ADAM TOOBY

OSPREY PUBLISHING
Bloomsbury Publishing Plc
Kemp House, Chawley Park, Cumnor Hill, Oxford OX2 9PH, UK
29 Earlsfort Terrace, Dublin 2, Ireland
1385 Broadway, 5th Floor, New York, NY 10018, USA
E-mail: info@ospreypublishing.com
www.ospreypublishing.com

OSPREY is a trademark of Osprey Publishing Ltd

First published in Great Britain in 2023

A catalogue record for this book is available from the British Library.

ISBN: PB 9781472854315; eBook 9781472854322;
ePDF 9781472854308; XML 9781472854339

23 24 25 26 27   10 9 8 7 6 5 4 3 2 1

Maps and diagrams by bounford.com
3D BEVs by Paul Kime
Index by Fionbar Lyons
Typeset by PDQ Digital Media Solutions, Bungay, UK
Printed and bound in India by Replika Press Private Ltd.

To find out more about our authors and books visit www.ospreypublishing.com. Here
you will find extracts, author interviews, details of forthcoming events and the option to
sign up for our newsletter.

Author's note:
I have used the World War II-era place
names in this book, some of which were
subsequently altered due to de-Staliniza-
tion. Most notably, Stalingrad itself
became "Volgograd" in 1961. Other
Soviet-era names have also changed from
Russian to Ukrainian spelling with the
emergence of the independent Ukrainian
state in 1991.

Author's dedication:
I would like to thank my wife Dorene,
son Alex, daughter Madeleine, and
daughter-in-law Ilona for their patience
and encouragement during my own
"Battle for Stalingrad" – the writing of
this book.

Glossary
ADD: *Aviatsiya dal'nego deystviya*
(Long-Range Aviation)
Fliegerkorps: Air Corps
Luftflotte: Air Fleet
PVO: *Voyska protivovozdushnoy oborony*
(Forces of Air Defense)
Stavka: Staff of the Supreme High
Command
VA: *Vozdushnya Armii* (Air Army)
VVS: *Voyenno-Vozdushnyye Sily*
(Soviet Air Force)

CONTENTS

ORIGINS 4

CHRONOLOGY 13

ATTACKER'S CAPABILITIES 17

DEFENDER'S CAPABILITIES 26

CAMPAIGN OBJECTIVES 35

THE CAMPAIGN 39

AFTERMATH AND ASSESSMENT 83

FURTHER READING 93

INDEX 95

ORIGINS

The road to Stalingrad

On November 23, 1942, the spearheads of the Soviet Don and Stalingrad Fronts met at Kalach, encircling the German Sixth Army. The next day, the first Luftwaffe Ju 52 transports took off carrying supplies for the Stalingrad pocket, launching the most strategically significant German air operation on the Eastern Front. Seventy-one days later, the frozen and starving remnants of the 250,000-man Sixth Army surrendered, marking the turning point of the war against the Third Reich. Despite the importance of the airlift, it is often only briefly addressed in accounts of the campaign, and its failure attributed to the winter weather. A closer analysis reveals that the air battle over Stalingrad marked a turning point in the air as well as in the conflict as a whole, as the experienced but exhausted Luftwaffe was defeated for the first time by a Soviet air arm with greatly improved organization, aircraft, and tactics.

The war in the east had begun with the VVS (Soviet Air Force) suffering devastating reverses as German forces captured millions of prisoners in vast encirclements and drove rapidly to the gates of Leningrad and Moscow. The pre-war Soviet Air Force was the largest in the world, but was crippled by poor leadership, organization, tactics, training, and readiness. The vast majority of the fighters and bombers stationed near the frontier were outclassed by the Bf 109s, Stukas, and bombers flown by veteran German pilots. The Luftwaffe's 2,770 frontline aircraft rapidly smashed the Soviet Air Force in a matter of weeks, with most VVS aircraft destroyed at their airfields before they could take off.

As the autumn turned into winter, the tyranny of distance, weather, and Red Army resistance slowed and ultimately halted the German advance. The exhausted and overstretched Luftwaffe was soon reduced to 30–50 percent aircraft readiness, with about 500 operational aircraft and only 15 percent of its 100,000 ground support vehicles still running. Operating from better airfields, with shorter supply lines and now receiving the first aircraft produced by industries evacuated by rail to the Urals, the VVS was able to renew the fight. Well prepared for winter operations, the Soviets had 1,000 operational aircraft on the Moscow front alone and were able to operate unimpeded by the Bf 109s and their veteran pilots. Stalin and the

Stavka initiated a series of counterattacks in front of Moscow that were soon expanded to a theater-wide offensive that inflicted massive losses on both sides but failed to inflict any decisive defeats on German forces.

The winter 1941–42 fighting included a Luftwaffe operation that would have a major impact on the subsequent Stalingrad campaign. In January, the Soviet counteroffensive against Army Group North encircled 95,000 German troops of the II and X Corps near the town of Demyansk and 5,500 troops 50 miles to the southwest at Kholm. The two positions prevented the Soviets from enveloping the bulk of Army Group North, and for the first time, an air force attempted to resupply a large ground force completely by air. Only 30 operational Ju 52 transports were available in the area in January, and the disorganized air supply effort initially fell far short of the pocket's supply requirements. The two corps needed 300 tons a day, including 54 tons of food and 21 tons of fuel, and the defenders often fired off 80–100 tons of artillery ammunition every day.

Luftwaffe air transport expert Oberst Fritz Morzik arrived to take charge on February 18 and immediately requested additional Ju 52s. He was given the bulk of the Ju 52 fleet and, with He 111 and Ju 86 bombers used to haul supplies, soon had almost 500 transports. Readiness in the primitive conditions was only around 30 percent, but the aircraft managed to deliver an average of 273 tons of supplies to the garrison each day. Over the next months the Ju 52s flew in 15,446 replacements and evacuated 22,093 sick and wounded. Kholm had no runway but was supplied by airdrop and large DFS 230 and Go 242 gliders landing with supplies. The VVS initially ignored the airlift and concentrated on attacking the troops defending the pocket, and the transports were able to fly in small groups and at low level. In March and April, the Soviets began to intercept the transports, and Morzik switched to flying larger groups at 6–8,000 feet with fighter escorts. Ju 52 losses declined from 52 in March to eight in April. The airlift was successful, but costly, with 106 Ju 52s, 17 He 111s, and two Ju 86s lost in total. Ground forces finally reached the pocket and opened a land supply corridor in May, although some air supply operations continued.

As the Soviet theater-wide attacks ground to a halt in the early spring of 1942, Hitler began to consider his options for a renewed summer offensive. The damaged German

German personnel servicing an He 111 bomber delivering supplies to Gumrak Airfield in the Stalingrad pocket, January, 1943. (Photo by ullstein bild/ ullstein bild via Getty Images)

OPPOSITE THE ROAD TO STALINGRAD: OPERATION *BLAU* AND THE FRONT LINE ON NOVEMBER 18, 1942

During early 1942, the Luftwaffe conducted the first large-scale aerial logistics operation in history, as it managed to resupply six divisions amounting to 95,000 soldiers surrounded by the Soviet winter offensive. The Luftwaffe's success at Demyansk played a role in persuading Hitler that it could similarly supply the Stalingrad pocket, although there the Sixth Army had over 250,000 troops. (Nik Cornish at www.Stavka.org.uk)

war machine could not repeat the theater-wide assault of 1941, so Hitler chose to mass resources in Army Group South for the primary 1942 effort. He settled on the Caucasus oilfields at Maikop, Grozny, and Baku as the primary targets, as their control would fuel the German war effort while crippling the Soviets. The plan for the offensive, codenamed Operation *Blau*, included an initial assault to destroy Soviet forces defending the front from Voronezh to Rostov, followed by subsequent exploitation on eastern and southeastern axes. Army Group South would split into two army groups. Army Group A would drive through Rostov to seize the Caucasus oilfields, while B drove to the east to secure its northern flank by holding the Don River and cutting the Volga at the city of Stalingrad. The Luftwaffe's 4th Air Fleet (*Luftflotte 4*) would provide air support to both axes of advance.

Before *Blau* could be launched, German forces had to clear the Crimea and capture Sevastopol. Brilliant attacks by General Erich von Manstein's Eleventh Army, ably supported by the 4th Air Fleet's VIII Air Corps, destroyed Soviet forces that had seized bridgeheads over the Kerch Straits in the Crimea in early 1942. The VIII Air Corps was led by the Luftwaffe's leading expert on close support operations, General Wolfram Freiherr von Richthofen. With the Kerch area secured, Manstein prepared to shift troops to assault Sevastopol, but Soviet forces launched an attack on May 11 aimed at the recapture of Kharkov north of the Crimea. VIII Air Corps elements rapidly shifted to support Army Group South's Operation *Fredericus* counteroffensive that cut off the attacking Soviet spearheads and handed the Soviets yet another defeat. With thousands of Red Army troops trudging to POW camps

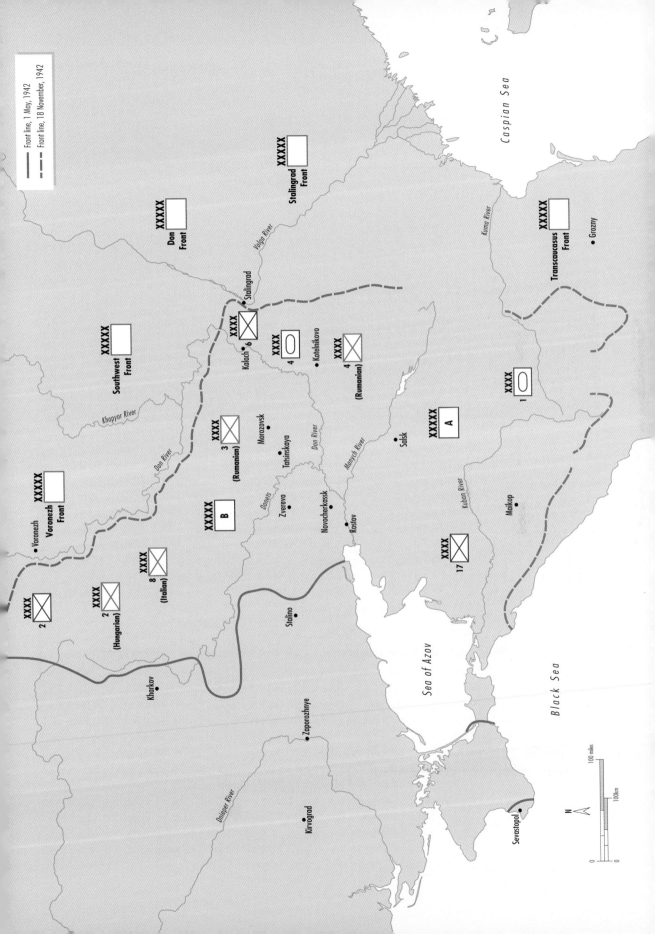

Front line, 1 May, 1942
Front line, 18 November, 1942

Caspian Sea

• Grozny

XXXXX
Transcaucasus
Front

Kuma River

XXXXX
Stalingrad
Front

Volga River

XXXXX
Don
Front

• Stalingrad

XXXX
6

• Kalach

XXXX
4

• Kotelnikovo

XXXX
4
(Rumanian)

XXXXX
Southwest
Front

Khopyor River

XXXX
3
(Rumanian)

• Morozovsk

• Tatsinskaya

Don River

Don River

Manych River

• Salsk

XXXXX
A

XXXX
1

XXXXX
Voronezh
Front

• Voronezh

XXXXX
B

Dnieper

• Zverevo

• Novocherkassk

• Rostov

Kuban River

• Maikop

XXXX
8
(Italian)

XXXX
2
(Hungarian)

XXXX
2

• Kharkov

• Stalino

XXXX
17

Sea of Azov

• Zaporozhnye

Dnieper River

• Kirvograd

Black Sea

• Sevastopol

N

100 miles
100km

Ju 87 Stuka dive-bombers. The 4th Air Fleet's VIII Air Corps was the most capable close air support force in the world in early 1942, having perfected its techniques during the early campaigns of the war. Unhindered by significant Soviet opposition in the air, its Stukas and bombers played a critical role in supporting Army Group South's counteroffensive at Kharkov and assault on Sevastopol in May–June, 1942. (Nik Cornish at www.Stavka.org.uk)

around Kharkov, Richthofen returned to the Sevastopol front and tightly integrated the Luftwaffe's bombers and Stukas into the Eleventh Army's fire and assault plan, serving as an extension of Manstein's massed artillery. Stukas and bombers flew multiple sorties each day, dropping 23,800 incendiary bombs and 2,264 tons of high explosives in five days as they blasted the attacking infantry through the Soviet defenses. Manstein won a field marshal's baton for the victory, and credited Richthofen's bombers and Stukas for a key role in the success. The Luftwaffe had been able to mass its forces to support the assault on Sevastopol and operated from well-established and well-supplied airfields in the Crimea close to their targets. The VVS was unable to mount much opposition, only managing 288 sorties and losing 141 aircraft to the Luftwaffe's 31. These unique advantages would not be seen again during the coming summer offensive.

Blau and Stalingrad

The German high command marshaled all available resources for Operation *Blau*. On the ground, Army Group South received 41 additional divisions – 21 of them from Germany's Hungarian, Italian, and Rumanian allies – and launched Operation *Blau* on June 28 with 1.3 million troops and 1,495 tanks. In the air, the 4th Air Fleet was reinforced by Luftwaffe units arriving from all over Europe. The 4th was ultimately able to field 1,700 aircraft, including 350 bombers, 211 fighters, 161 Bf 110 heavy fighters (*Zerstörer*), 150 Stuka dive-bombers, and 91 attack (*Schlacht*) types. Twelve hundred of the force was operational at the start of the offensive. Richthofen, now in command of the 4th Air Fleet, directed his subordinate IV Air Corps to conduct longer range interdiction attacks while the VIII Air Corps under General der Flieger Martin Fiebig specialized in close support to the troops. Army Groups North and Center would hold the line with weakened ground forces. Only 600 Luftwaffe combat aircraft were assigned to Army Group Center, and 575 with Army Group North. Stalin and the Stavka high command remained convinced, however, that Operation *Blau* was a feint and retained the bulk of Soviet ground and VVS resources to defend Moscow.

Blau began with rapid progress, and Axis forces soon battled to Voronezh and Rostov. The veteran pilots of the 4th Air Fleet inflicted heavy losses on their VVS opponents, and its Stukas, Ju 88s, and He 111s were able to provide powerful support to German ground forces largely unchallenged by enemy fighters. The newly formed VVS 8th Air Army possessed 454 aircraft to defend the southern front when *Blau* began, but its poorly trained pilots suffered heavy losses and by October the 8th was reduced to 188 planes, only 24 of them fighters.

Convinced by *Blau*'s initial successes that the USSR was nearing collapse, Hitler accelerated the operation's timetable. Rather than securing the northern flank on the Don before thrusting south toward the oilfields, he dispatched Army Groups B and A on simultaneous offensives against their distant objectives on the Volga and deep in the Caucasus. The panzer spearheads moved forward but with lengthening lines of communication and limited logistical support struggled to reach their distant objectives. A vast gap opened in the Kalmyk Steppe between the two army groups. Army Group A's panzers seized the Maikop oilfields, and mountain troops planted the swastika flag on Mount Elbrus in the Caucasus, but the Maikop fields had been sabotaged and the panzer thrust finally ground to a halt in front of Grozny. The main prize of Baku remained over 300 miles distant.

Army Group B drove east to secure the line of the Don while Group A struggled in the Caucasus. In the original *Blau* plan the city of Stalingrad was a secondary objective. Its seizure would anchor the Don River flank defenses and allow the Axis to interdict river traffic on the Volga. By August the Sixth Army was able to establish a bridgehead across the Don and mount an attack east, but the initial rapid thrusts into Stalingrad were hindered by strong counterattacks from the north and stubborn Soviet resistance. Richthofen supported the assault, with 600 bombers launching 2,000 sorties against Stalingrad during the night of August 23/24. More than half of the bomb loads were incendiaries, leading to devastating

Stuka over Stalingrad, August, 1942. Richthofen massed his 4th Air Fleet bomber force and launched a series of devastating bombing raids on Stalingrad on August 23 and 24. (Photo by ullstein bild/ullstein bild via Getty Images)

fires, but the Soviet troops used the ruined urban landscape to force the Sixth Army to fight what the Germans called *Rattenkrieg*, the "war of the rats" – grinding and costly house-to-house combat that negated their superior armor and firepower.

General Alexander Novikov, recently appointed to command the VVS, had just arrived in Stalingrad to orchestrate VVS support but survived the August 23–24 raid and immediately took measures to support the struggle of Vasily Chuikov's 62nd Army to cling to the city. He called in the newly formed 16th and 17th Air Armies to reinforce the weakened 8th, and directed the construction of large numbers of airfields to the east of the Volga. Twenty-four operational and 19 decoy fields were eventually built for the 8th Air Army alone. Despite these efforts, the Luftwaffe maintained air superiority during the fall, and Novikov concentrated on husbanding his strength. Soviet air operations were limited to small-scale aerial "zasada" ambush attacks against isolated German aircraft, night bombing operations by ADD (Long-Range Aviation) Il-4s, and harassing raids by PO-2 biplanes serving in night bomber regiments.

Over the next three months, Hitler became fixated on the complete seizure of Stalingrad and ordered more and more Wehrmacht and Luftwaffe resources dedicated to a series of costly assaults to fully secure the Volga riverbank. Richthofen's limited air resources had been spread thin trying to support the Army Group A and B spearheads hundreds of kilometers distant, continually shifting its aircraft to support small opportunities as they arose. As the assaults on the city continued, the 4th Air Fleet ultimately concentrated 1,000 aircraft to support the Sixth Army attacks. Richthofen bragged of delivering bombs "within grenade throwing" distance of the troops, but the impact of the repeated strikes on the same targets in the city was uncertain, and the Luftwaffe bombers repeatedly hitting the city were unable to attack the Caucasus oilfields, originally the primary objective of the summer offensive. Grozny remained just beyond the panzers' reach, and Baku, which alone provided 80 percent of the USSR's oil supplies, was untouched. Hitler authorized some raids on the oilfields in October, but by this time VVS resistance in the Caucasus had stiffened.

Operation *Uranus*

Stalin and the Soviet high command were not content to hold the Germans at Grozny and Stalingrad, and since September had been planning a winter counteroffensive. The Sixth Army's assaults in Stalingrad left the protection of its long flanks to the Rumanian Third and Fourth Armies. The Axis allies lacked adequate anti-tank capabilities and reserves, and the Soviets retained several bridgeheads over the Don River from which to launch the offensive. The Soviet Stavka high command had fed in just enough force to allow Chuikov to hold General Friedrich Paulus in Stalingrad, and while the overall front-wide balance of forces was similar, the Red Army was able to mass its forces to outmatch the Rumanians in the key attack sectors north and south of the city by a heavy margin: 13,540 artillery pieces and mortars and 894 tanks ensured that the attackers would rapidly overpower the defenders. The *Uranus* plan included strong air support from Novikov's VVS.

Luftwaffe reconnaissance identified the Soviet build-up on the Don, but Hitler remained adamant that the 4th Air Fleet continue to focus its resources against the few positions still held by the Red Army in Stalingrad. On November 11, the VIII Air Corps launched large-scale Stuka raids to support what turned out to be the final German assault in the city. By late November, the 4th Air Fleet's men and machines had been profoundly weakened by the demands of the long summer campaign and limited logistical support. Some of its units were detached and sent to the Mediterranean to respond to the November 8 Allied *Torch* landings.

Balance of aviation forces November 19–20, 1942					
Unit	Commander	Supporting	Combat aircraft	Operational combat aircraft	Comments
4th Air Fleet	Richthofen	Army Groups A, B	732	402	
Axis total			732	402	
8th Air Army	General-Mayor Timofey Khryukin	Stalingrad Front	499	267	
16th Air Army	General-Mayor Sergey Rudenko	Don Front	303	229	Formed November 16
17th Air Army	General-Mayor Stepan Krasovsky	Southwestern Front	423	377	
Soviet total *Uranus*			1,225	873	
2nd Air Army	General-Mayor Konstantin Smirnov	Voronezh Front	163	139	Operating to north of offensive
102nd Air Defense Division	Commander I. G. Puntus	Stalingrad area	88	23	Available to support
Soviet total*			1,476	1,035	
*Bombers of Long-Range Aviation (ADD) were also available to support.					

On November 19, a massive Soviet artillery barrage hit the Rumanian Third Army positions along the Don, heralding the launch of Operation *Uranus*. Despite German claims to the contrary, the Rumanians initially put up strong resistance, but within hours their front began to collapse in the face of heavy Soviet tank and infantry assaults. The weak XXXXVIII Panzer Corps in reserve was unable to halt the Red Army advance, and an 80-mile gap was torn in the Axis defensive front. By 2200 hours on the 19th, Paulus was alarmed enough to halt all attacks in the city and begin to look to the security of his flanks.

The Luftwaffe's massive air raids in August created a ruined urban landscape that proved ideal for Soviet infantry defenders. The Soviet high command fed in just enough assets to drain the resources of the Sixth Army, while massing a powerful counterattack force to hit the weak Axis flanks. (Courtesy of the Central Museum of the Armed Forces, Moscow, via Stavka)

Soviet planning for Operation *Uranus* included preparations for strong air support, but poor weather during the early hours of the attack grounded most of the VVS Shturmoviks. Soviet artillery and armor superiority allowed them to rapidly break through the poorly equipped Rumanian Third and Fourth Army defenders. (Courtesy of the Central Museum of the Armed Forces, Moscow, via Stavka)

The Soviet high command had prepared heavy air support for the *Uranus* attack, but poor weather hindered air operations by both sides for days. Icy runways, mist, snow, and a low cloud ceiling on the 19th kept the VVS from executing its full strike plan. Despite the conditions, VIII Air Corps commander Martin Fiebig ordered all available Stuka and Hs 123 and Hs 129 attack aircraft to assist the Rumanians. Hans-Ulrich Rudel, the highly decorated tank-killing ace, led his Stuka squadron into the air, overflying fleeing Rumanians who had succumbed to "tank panic" and striking Soviet cavalry and tank units threatening his own airfield. Overall, the Luftwaffe managed 120 sorties while the Soviet 17th VA (Air Army) flew 546 and the 16th VA 82.

On the 20th, General Andrey Yeremenko's Stalingrad Front launched the southern portion of the offensive and rapidly broke through the Rumanian Fourth Army to its front. The poor weather kept Luftwaffe reconnaissance aircraft grounded, and the Germans were unable to track the fluid situation threatening the Sixth Army's rear areas. Two recon He 111s were lost attempting to fly on the 20th. On the 23rd, a Soviet tank detachment seized the key bridge at Kalach when the German defenders misidentified the unit approaching with lights blazing and at speed as friendly, and the Don and Stalingrad Fronts soon established contact. The VVS was able to conduct 1,000 sorties from the 19th to the 22nd, most of them by Il-2 Shturmovik attack aircraft, and the Axis 361. Stukas flew 141 of these sorties to help the Rumanians, losing five Ju 87s. With clearing weather on the 24th, the 8th, 16th, and 17th VAs increased their operations tempo and conducted 6,000 sorties over the next seven days.

Luftwaffe personnel posted behind the front line began hasty efforts to evacuate operational aircraft and ground support equipment as others were formed into ad hoc ground units to defend their airfields. Karpovka Airfield was hastily abandoned on the 23rd as the Soviet 44th Mechanized Corps approached. At Oblivskaya Airfield, headquarters of the VIII Air Corps, Colonel Reiner Stahel of the 99th Flak Regiment formed a battle group from Flak, field police, supply, signal, and even kitchen battalion elements to defend the base and a nearby rail crossing. Battle Group Stahel would hold the line for weeks, winning its commander promotion to Generalleutnant in January, 1943.

The closing of the Soviet pincers encircled Paulus' Sixth Army, Rumanian remnants, a corps of the Fourth Panzer Army, and most of the 9th Luftwaffe Flak Division. The Soviets soon learned that rather than the expected 95,000, they had in fact surrounded a force of over 250,000 troops, along with approximately 100 tanks, 2,000 guns, and 10,000 trucks. Hitler ordered that the Sixth Army begin to shift forces to form a 360-degree defense, and attention now focused on the fate of the forces encircled in the Stalingrad pocket. The answer would decide the fate of Hitler's 1942 campaign and, ultimately, the German war in the east.

CHRONOLOGY

1941

June 22–December 31 Operation *Barbarossa*. The Luftwaffe rapidly destroys the poorly prepared Soviet Air Force, with Soviet aircraft losses totaling 20,000 by December.

1942

Winter Wehrmacht's Operation *Typhoon* grinds to a halt at the gates of Moscow. Soviet forces begin a winter counteroffensive against Army Group Center, driving it back but failing to destroy it in large part because of Hitler's "stand fast" orders. Exhaustion and severe winter weather allow the VVS to renew its challenge to the exhausted Luftwaffe.

January 5 Stalin orders the Moscow counteroffensive be expanded into a series of front-wide offensives dissipating and weakening the force of the attacks. With both sides exhausted, Soviet operations come to a halt in late February and Luftwaffe forces are slowly able to rebuild and reinforce with fresh units.

February 19–May 18 The Luftwaffe assembles a force of 500 transports to fly supplies to 95,000 troops cut off north of Moscow at Demyansk and Kholm. While costly, the airlift succeeds and, despite low transport aircraft readiness rates, delivers an average of 273 tons of supplies daily.

April 5 Hitler issues Führer Directive No. 41 with directions for the Operation *Blau* summer offensive. Army Group South will destroy Soviet forces and then divide into two forces: Army Group B will seize and hold a defensive line anchored on the Don River, while Army Group A drives deep into the Caucasus to seize the Maikop, Grozny, and Baku oilfields. The Luftwaffe's 4th Air Fleet will support both army groups.

May 8 Erich von Manstein's Eleventh Army, supported by the VIII Air Corps under Richthofen, destroys the Soviet bridgehead on the Kerch Peninsula in the Crimea.

May 12 The Soviets launch an ambitious offensive to retake Kharkov; five days later, Army Group South launches a counterattack, Operation *Fredericus*, that cuts off and destroys the attacking force. Luftwaffe elements rapidly deploy from the Crimea to support the counterattack, and then return to support Manstein's assault on Sevastopol.

June 28 Operation *Blau* begins with attacks to seize Voronezh; Stalin and the Soviet high command retain most reserves to protect Moscow, which they believe to be the true German objective in 1942. The Luftwaffe secures air superiority, and its bomber and strike aircraft operate with impunity.

July 4 Sevastopol falls to Manstein's Eleventh Army, closely supported by Luftwaffe air strikes.

July 9 Hitler activates Army Groups A and B.

July 18 Richthofen assumes command of the 4th Air Fleet; General Martin Fiebig becomes VIII Air Corps commander.

July 23 German forces capture Rostov, and Hitler, believing the USSR is on the brink of collapse, issues Führer Directive No. 45 to accelerate the *Blau* timetable and simultaneously launch Army Group A into the Caucasus, while Army Group B, led by Paulus' Sixth Army, is sent to secure Stalingrad. The 4th Air Fleet struggles to support these two distant advances on a front now hundreds of miles long.

August–November The German offensive gains ground but fails to achieve any of *Blau*'s strategic objectives. Army Group A reaches and seizes the Maikop oilfields on August 9, but they have been destroyed by the retreating Soviets. Its attack toward Grozny bogs down in front of the city due to logistical shortages and enemy resistance. Paulus' Sixth Army attack into Stalingrad makes initial progress but soon deteriorates into costly house-to-house urban combat. At Hitler's insistence, German forces launch major offensives to clear the remaining enemy-held portions of the city on September 14, 27, and October 14, supported by the bulk of the 4th Air Fleet's aircraft. Weaker Axis allied units are posted to defend the Sixth Army's flanks.

November 8 Allied Operation *Torch* landings in French North Africa begin. Hitler responds by shifting Luftwaffe resources from the Eastern Front to the Mediterranean. Ultimately, a third of the total 750 Ju 52 transport force will be used to transport 81,000 troops into Tunisia to hold a bridgehead in Africa.

November 19–20 The Soviets launch Operation *Uranus*. The Southwest Front under Vatutin supported by Rokossovsky's Don Front attack from the north, destroying the Rumanian Third Army, and the next day Yeremenko's Stalingrad Front smashes through the Rumanian Fourth Army to the south of the city.

November 20 Hitler directs Manstein to command a newly activated Army Group Don to stabilize the situation and directs the Sixth Army to stay in place and be supplied by the Luftwaffe until it can be relieved.

November 21 Hitler orders Paulus to stand fast in Stalingrad, even if encircled.

November 23 The Soviet pincers meet on the 23rd, and Paulus' Sixth Army is encircled with over 250,000 troops. Poor weather limits both sides' air operations, with the VVS managing about 200 sorties daily, and the Luftwaffe about half that number. The lack of air reconnaissance hinders Axis ability to track the situation,

and their sorties focus on the defense of their own airfields.

November 24–25 The Stalingrad airlift begins but is only able to deliver small amounts of supplies. Richthofen's 4th Air Fleet is placed in overall command of the effort and begins to reorganize after evacuating forward airfields and receiving additional transport units.

November 30 Richthofen puts Fiebig and VIII Air Corps in direct control of the air supply operation. Fiebig concentrates his Ju 52s and Ju 86s at Tatsinskaya and He 111s at Morozovsk.

December 4 Soviet Air Force Commander Novikov establishes a system of air blockade zones to organize VVS efforts to halt the Luftwaffe airlift.

December 7 The airlift's best day; 135 transports land at Pitomnik Airfield in the pocket, delivering 362.2 tons of supplies, but weather conditions prevent any flights on the 3rd and the 9th.

The Luftwaffe's response to the *Uranus* attack was limited by poor weather, but Stuka ace Hans-Ulrich Rudel was able to lead his squadron in a series of attacks on the 5th Tank Army as it penetrated the Rumanian lines. (Nik Cornish at www.Stavka.org.uk)

German Stukas and He 111s were used throughout the fall for repeated strikes on Stalingrad as the Sixth Army battled to drive the last Soviet defenders across the Volga. The He 111s would have been better employed on attacks on the Soviet oil infrastructure at Grozny and Baku in the Caucasus. (Nik Cornish at www.Stavka.org.uk)

December 12 Manstein launches Operation *Winter Storm* (*Wintergewitter*) to relieve the Stalingrad pocket; on order, Paulus' Sixth Army is to launch Operation *Thunderclap* (*Donnerschlag*) to strike south and meet the relieving LVII Panzer Corps. Richthofen has to divert some fighters, Stukas, and bombers from the airlift to support the relief attack.

Mid-December German fighters are unable to escort the transports in daily through the Soviet air blockade's fighter defenses. Luftwaffe decides to cancel daylight flights in good weather and rely on flights at night or in cloudy conditions to try to avoid interception.

December 16 Soviet Operation *Little Saturn* begins against the Italian Eighth Army, which collapses after three days. Soviet tank corps exploit the penetration and begin to move to raid the major German airlift airfields at Tatsinskaya and Morozovsk. Manstein gambles that the *Winter Storm* force can break through to Stalingrad before the Soviet forces take the airfields.

December 19–23 Heavily supported by the 4th Air Fleet's bombers and Stukas, the LVII Panzer Corps' *Winter Storm* attack reaches the Myskova River, 35 miles from the Stalingrad pocket. Manstein urges that the Sixth Army launch Operation *Thunderclap* to link up with the relieving force, but Hitler insists that it not abandon its positions in Stalingrad. Hitler promises more divisions to reinforce the relieving force and allow it to reach the pocket, but some of them will not arrive for weeks.

December 24, 1942–January 1, 1943 Tatsinskaya Airfield is overrun by Soviet armor on December 24. 108 Ju 52s and 16 Ju 86s escape under fire, but 50 aircraft, along with the supplies and most of the maintenance equipment at the base, are destroyed. Soviet armor is unable to overrun Morozovsk and is hit hard by German air attack, but that airfield is also abandoned in early January. The airlift now operates from bases further from the pocket – Ju 52s from Salsk and He 111s from Novocherkassk.

December 28 As the Soviets continue to attack toward Rostov, Hitler finally allows Army Group A to begin to withdraw from the Caucasus.

1943

January 3–14 With Soviet forces threatening Salsk, Fiebig orders construction of a new fallback airfield for his Ju 52s. The Luftwaffe builds the airfield on a frozen cornfield at Zverevo.

January 9 Paulus refuses a Soviet surrender demand from Marshals Voronov and Rokossovsky.

January 10 The Red Army launches the Operation *Koltso* ("Ring") offensive to crush the Sixth Army.

January 13 The Soviets launch the Voronezh–Kharkov offensive on the upper Don, rapidly destroying the defending Second Hungarian Army. At this point Soviet forces are closer to Rostov than most of the retreating Army Group Don and A forces.

Soviet Pe-2 light bombers in flight. The VVS found itself driven from the skies by a revitalized Luftwaffe 4th Air Fleet during the summer campaign, but with the onset of Operation *Uranus*, Soviet attack and bomber aviation returned to daylight operations in force. (Courtesy of the Central Museum of the Armed Forces, Moscow, via Stavka)

January 16 The main German airfield in the pocket at Pitomnik airfield is overrun by Soviet forces. Airlift operations shift to Gumrak, which has been kept unprepared by the Sixth Army to avoid drawing attention to its main headquarters located nearby. The Ju 52 force evacuates Salsk and arrives at the newly built and poorly equipped airfield at Zverevo. Field Marshal and deputy Luftwaffe Commander Milch arrives at 4th Air Fleet headquarters, ordered by Hitler to take any measures necessary to improve the airlift.

January 19 Novocherkassk Airfield evacuated.

January 23 Gumrak is overrun by Soviet forces, leaving airdrop the only method for the Luftwaffe resupply of the pocket.

January 31 Paulus surrenders the southern pocket holding out in the ruins of Stalingrad.

February 2 The last organized resistance in Stalingrad is eliminated.

February 7 Zverevo is evacuated.

February–March The Third Battle of Kharkov: Red Army spearheads attacking into Ukraine are cut off and Kharkov retaken during Manstein's "backhand blow" counterattack, ending the Soviet winter offensive.

February–March German transports successfully resupply the German Seventeenth Army in the Kuban bridgehead from bases in southern Ukraine and Crimea. With the spring thaw, resupply by sea is possible and most transport units are withdrawn for refitting.

ATTACKER'S CAPABILITIES

The Luftwaffe on the Eastern Front

Doctrine, tactics, and logistics

Air combat on the Eastern Front was heavily focused on support to ground operations, with strategic bombing largely limited to small-scale Soviet raids on Berlin and German bombing of Moscow in the war's first months. The Luftwaffe's approach to air war – *Operativer Luftkrieg* or Operational Air War – was focused on aiding ground force operations but included more than pure close air support. Its first objective was to secure air superiority both by attacking enemy airfields and intercepting enemy aircraft aloft to allow its strike aircraft to operate. Once able to concentrate on ground targets, the Luftwaffe's conception of support to the army included a strong focus on interdiction, including attacks on targets deep behind the front, ranging from lines of communication to reserve troops.

The Luftwaffe maintained a strong qualitative edge over its Soviet opponents throughout the summer and autumn of 1942. Its pilots and ground personnel were battle hardened and its units well organized, flexible, and mobile. Each air fleet had organic motorized ground columns and airfield construction companies to support rapid advances. German aircraft were superior to the obsolescent aircraft that equipped many VVS units in early 1942, and the latest G "Gustav" models of the Bf 109 fighters arriving in the summer maintained a technological edge even over the modern Soviet Yak-1, La-5, and LaGG-3 fighters. The Luftwaffe employed superior tactics, with their pilots using the deadly finger-four *Rotte* formation of two pairs (*Schwarm*), each of a leader and wingman. VVS pilots were slow to abandon the *Katte* formation of three aircraft in a "vic," which proved inflexible and extremely vulnerable to the Bf 109s.

The Luftwaffe's weaknesses were born of its strengths. Throughout the 1930s the Luftwaffe had focused on the creation of combat units and neglected the logistical and maintenance structure needed for sustained operations. Organized for rapid, concentrated offensive operations and high mobility, German air fleets were much less able to cope with the drawn-out attritional combat that it faced in the USSR. As the advance into the Soviet Union

Each Luftwaffe air fleet had highly mobile ground elements capable of rapidly following advancing German forces and setting up new, lightly equipped airfields to keep air support up with the troops. This system was unable to sustain the Luftwaffe when the campaign in the Soviet Union bogged down into a protracted battle of attrition. (Photo by Atlantic-Press/ullstein bild via Getty Images)

German troops in winter gear occupy shallow trench positions. The Soviet encirclement forced Paulus to reorient his troops to mount a 360-degree "hedgehog" defense. The Soviet high command assessed that 90,000–95,000 troops were in the pocket, but soon discovered the force was two to three times that size. (Nik Cornish at www.Stavka.org.uk)

bogged down, the Luftwaffe was unable to concentrate on a few key axes of advance and was forced to spread out to cover a vast front. While the 4th Air Fleet could mass its bombers and Stukas to support the assault on Sevastopol during the summer of 1942, by the autumn it had to operate on a front hundreds of miles in length stretching from Voronezh to Stalingrad and down to the Caucasus.

Logistical planning took second place to operational demands in German military culture and were a Luftwaffe weakness throughout the campaign on the Eastern Front. The combination of supply shortages, aircraft and aircrew exhaustion, and weather so weakened the Luftwaffe during the winter of 1941–42 that the VVS was able to regain its footing and challenge the Germans over Moscow and during Stalin's winter offensive. As the war stretched into a second year, the Luftwaffe had difficulty maintaining its forward airbases, a problem made more severe as the summer offensive drove the 4th Air Fleet farther from established sources of supply. Maintenance was also a challenge, as the quick campaigns of 1939 and 1940 allowed the Luftwaffe to operate with a lean maintenance infrastructure at the front, with any aircraft needing complex repairs sent back to the Reich.

In November, 1942, the summer advance had left the 4th Air Fleet to operate on poorly equipped airfields at the end of a long and low-capacity single track rail supply line. A distance of 217 miles separated the major theater railhead at Stalino and the German front line, and only a small number of low-capacity rail lines and a poor road network were available to move supplies up to the troops. Twelve trains could transit to the Stalingrad area each day, and only one and a half of these were assigned to the Luftwaffe. As a result, the 4th Air Fleet's bases had minimal infrastructure and support equipment, and aircraft serviceability rates declined over the fall from about 75 percent at the start of *Blau* to below 50 percent in November. With ground force supply needs a priority for rail transport,

Richthofen relied on the 4th Air Fleet's organic Ju 52s to get aviation fuel and other Luftwaffe supplies to the forward airfields. Transport readiness averaged 30–40 percent, even lower than the combat elements.

Richthofen's 4th Air Fleet

The Luftwaffe was organized into air fleets (*Luftflotte*), similar in size and role to US numbered air forces. Four were in existence in 1939, and by the end of the war an additional three had been formed. Luftwaffe air fleets were self-contained commands controlling all types of combat aircraft as well as support, anti-aircraft (Flak), and signals elements. Each army group on the Eastern Front was supported by an air fleet. Air fleets typically controlled one or two air corps (*Fliegerkorps*), operational-level formations that varied widely in composition depending on role and mission, but typically controlled 350–600 combat aircraft in the early years of the war. The air corps in turn controlled a variable number of wings (*Geschwader*), which at full strength had roughly 90 aircraft. The wings consisted of three 30-plane air groups (*Gruppe*), each with three squadrons (*Staffeln*) with a headquarters and nine aircraft each. Luftflotte headquarters could organize ad hoc air divisions for special tasks, and during the airlift campaign, Richthofen created one such unit to cover the Caucasus and another to cover the Don while the VIII and IV Air Corps operated in the Stalingrad area.

Types of Luftwaffe Air Wings (*Geschwader*)			
Aircraft	German designation	Abbreviation	Translation
Fighters	*Jagdgeschwader*	JG	Fighter Wing
Bombers	*Kampfgeschwader*	KG	Bomber Wing
Dive-bombers	*Stukageschwader*	St. G	Stuka Wing
Attack aircraft	*Schlachtgeschwader*	Sch. G	Ground Attack Wing
Bf 110s	*Zerstörergeschwader*	ZG	Destroyer Wing

The 4th Air Fleet was the key Luftwaffe force during the Stalingrad campaign. In November, 1942, Generaloberst Wolfram Freiherr von Richthofen controlled 732 combat

A highly energetic commander, Richthofen would use his light Storch liaison aircraft to visit multiple headquarters daily to ensure the best possible coordination of air and ground operations. Richthofen was promoted to Generalfeldmarschall by Hitler on February 15, 1943 but was moved to reserve status due to health issues and died in 1945. (Nik Cornish at www.Stavka.org.uk)

aircraft of which 401, or 55 percent, were operational in late November. The 4th was led by an experienced command team. Richthofen was a relation of the Red Baron and a World War I ace with eight victories. Initially Richthofen was cautious about the use of the Luftwaffe for close support of ground troops, but while serving as chief of staff of the Condor Legion in Spain became a convert and pioneered the use of Stuka dive-bombers in the role. He commanded the VIII Air Corps in 1940–41 in the west and Balkans campaigns and fought to help Army Group Center defend against the Soviet winter offensive during the Battle for Moscow. Transferred to the south, Richthofen's strike aircraft made a decisive contribution to Manstein's assault on Sevastopol, before assuming command of the 4th Air Fleet on June 23. Richthofen was an energetic, ruthless, and forceful personality. He led from the front, often visiting several air and ground headquarters a day via his light Storch aircraft when coordinating high-intensity operations. General Martin Fiebig led the VIII Air Corps which was supporting Paulus' Sixth Army as it tried to drive the Soviets out of their last toeholds in Stalingrad. General Kurt Pflugbeil's weaker IV Air Corps was providing air support to Army Group A's stalled offensive in the Caucasus. The 25th Air Administrative Command controlled ground services support to the air fleet from its headquarters in Rostov. In the German military, the Luftwaffe controlled anti-aircraft assets, and the 4th Air Fleet's I Anti-Aircraft Artillery Corps consisted of two divisions, the 15th and 9th. Operations by the 4th Air Fleet throughout 1942 had demonstrated flexibility, mobility, and hitting power, although it had not conducted large-scale air transport operations.

Luftwaffe fighters

The 4th Air Fleet's order of battle included the 3rd and 52nd Fighter Wings (*Jagdgeschwader*) equipped with Bf 109s. The 109 was the dominant fighter aircraft in the east during 1941 and 1942 and outclassed the obsolete Soviet I-16 and I-153 fighters shot down in large numbers during *Barbarossa* and still in the VVS in some numbers in early 1942. Bf 109 units upgraded from the F to G "Gustav" model in the summer of 1942, and its more powerful engine ensured a measure of technical superiority even over the more modern Soviet Yak-1 and La-5 fighters.

Veteran *Experten* pilots with hundreds of combat sorties, radios in every plane, and advanced finger-four *Rotte-Schwarm* tactics gave the Luftwaffe a decisive edge in the summer and fall. The Soviet practice of rushing poorly trained aircrew to the front to keep numbers up led to German aces achieving large numbers of air victories. As the Luftwaffe did not rotate pilots out of frontline duty, huge scores were ultimately achieved by the surviving aces. By 1945, 107 German pilots had shot down more than 100, 15 more than 200, and two – Erich Hartmann and Gerhard Barkhorn – over 300 enemy aircraft.

The 4th Air Fleet's 3rd and 52nd Fighter Wings had limited numbers of fighters and pilots available in November and had to carefully choose where to concentrate their combat power. Having begun *Blau* in June with 325 Bf 109s, by late November the 4th Air Fleet was down to 203, of which only 125 were operational. 53rd and 77th Fighter Wings were dispatched from the USSR and sent to the Mediterranean in early November, and the VIII Air Corps supporting operations in the Stalingrad area had fewer than 50 operational fighters at the start of the Soviet offensive. With the recall of most of the fighters from tasks with Army Group A, roughly 90 were assembled in late November to support the airlift. 4th Air Fleet also controlled a single wing of Bf 110 *Zerstörer* (destroyer) fighters that had longer range but were less maneuverable in combat.

Bombers and ground attack

The Luftwaffe had pioneered close air support operations during the Spanish Civil War and perfected them during 1939–42. German doctrine for ground forces support encompassed

The Bf 109 was the dominant fighter on the Eastern Front for the first years of the war. Soviet Yak-1 and La-5 fighters were able to compete with the 109E and F models, but the G "Gustavs" that arrived at the front in the summer of 1942 had superior speed. (Photo by Photo12/Universal Images Group via Getty Images)

air superiority and interdiction tasks in addition to direct attacks on enemy ground targets. Luftwaffe liaison officers, designated *Fliegerverbindungsoffiziere* or "Flivos," were placed with ground headquarters at most levels, typically down to the division in 1942, and air strikes could take place in as little as two hours after the request. In fluid operations, advancing Wehrmacht units typically had to use flags on their vehicles and colored panels or smoke to mark positions and avoid attacks by their own aircraft, but Richthofen had begun the practice of having Stuka pilots accompany panzer columns for better control of air strikes. Luftwaffe close air support reached its apogee under Richthofen and Manstein during the assault on Sevastopol. The VIII Air Corps strove to match this success during the repeated

OPPOSITE LUFTWAFFE TRANSPORT CAPABILITIES

assaults on Stalingrad although the result was less successful. The blunt Richthofen was vocal in his criticism of the ground forces, claiming they lacked aggression and did not follow up the air strikes rapidly enough.

A force of 155 Ju 87D Stuka dive-bombers gave the 4th Air Fleet the capability for pinpoint accuracy. The Stuka dive-bombers had been vulnerable to the RAF in 1940 but remained effective in the east, particularly when the fighters had secured air superiority. Although frequently used to directly support ground troops, the Luftwaffe also employed them against targets farther behind enemy lines requiring high accuracy. A relatively small portion of Luftwaffe wings were attack (*Schlacht*) units dedicated to support operations for the ground troops. The single attack wing assigned to the 4th Air Fleet comprised 18 Bf 109 fighter bombers and 25 Hs 123/129 specialized ground attack aircraft. The 4th Air Fleet controlled a total of 123 capable He 111 twin-engine medium bombers in its 27th and 55th Bomber Wings (*Kampfgeschwader*). He 111s would also prove critical when used in the transport role during the airlift. The versatile 147 Ju 88s of the 1st and 51st Bomber Wings could perform a variety of tasks, including level and dive-bombing. Like the fighter pilots, most Luftwaffe bomber and Stuka crews were veterans. Hans-Ulrich Rudel, commander of a squadron in the 2nd Stuka Group during the campaign, flew his 1,000th sortie in February, 1943.

Reconnaissance

Reconnaissance was a major German advantage during 1942, and the 4th Air Fleet contained a variety of aircraft for the purpose, including Fw 189s, Do 17s, and Ju 88s. Light

A Luftwaffe Bf 110 fighter in 1942. The 4th Air Fleet contained over 50 Bf 110s in its 1st *Zerstörer* (Destroyer) Wing. Pulled back from support to Army Group A in the Caucasus due to the Soviet *Uranus* offensive, the pilots of the 1st found themselves used as a "fire brigade," to meet different crises at the front. (Photo by PhotoQuest/ Getty Images)

Luftwaffe transport capabilities

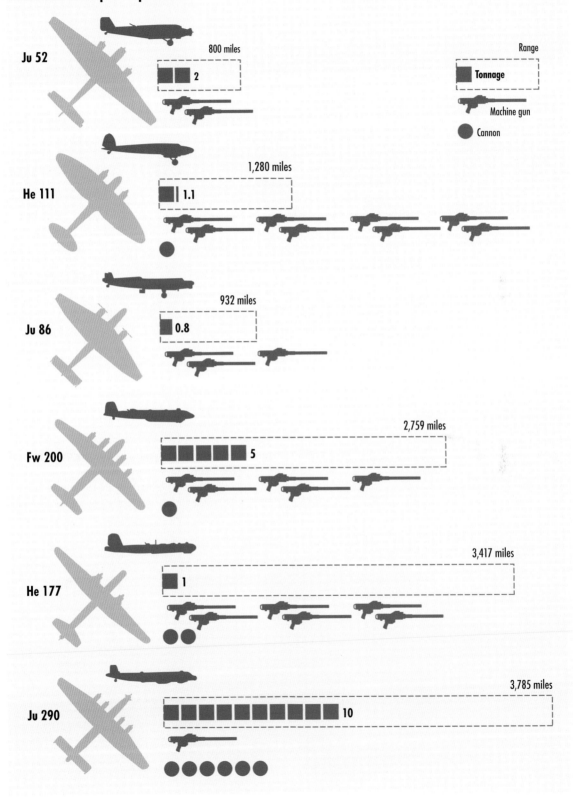

Ju 52
800 miles
2

Range
Tonnage
Machine gun
Cannon

He 111
1,280 miles
1.1

Ju 86
932 miles
0.8

Fw 200
2,759 miles
5

He 177
3,417 miles
1

Ju 290
3,785 miles
10

reconnaissance aircraft used for tactical reconnaissance and artillery spotting were attached to and controlled by the ground forces in a rare instance of Göring's Luftwaffe not keeping all aviation assets under its direct control.

Transports

Richthofen's 4th Air Fleet contained around 275 transport planes when *Uranus* began, with 146 operational. The VIII Air Corps controlled the 50th and 102nd Special Duty Bomber Wings (*Kampfgruppe zu besonderen Verwendung*) with Ju 52s, and the 5th Special Duty Bomber Group with He 111s dedicated to the transport role. The 4th Air Fleet directly controlled additional Ju 52s in the 90th Group, and some were assigned to the 25th Air Administrative Command. The He 111 bombers of the 55th and 27th Bomber Wings could also be shifted to transportation duties.

These transports were well worn from intensive operations throughout the summer. Due to the limitations of the single-track rail link from Rostov to the front, the 4th relied on its Ju 52s to fly its aviation fuel, ammunition, and other supplies to its forward airfields. Between August and October over 20,000 tons of aviation fuel went to supply the 4th's airfields, while an additional 4,614 tons was flown to the ground troops. Return flights were used to evacuate 51,619 Sixth Army wounded. Ju 52 operational readiness was often well below the combat aircraft's 50 percent rate due to the high demand for resupply flights. On November 25, Richthofen could only get 33 Ju 52s in the air for the very first supply runs into the pocket.

Anti-aircraft (Flak) units

A Ju 52 on a muddy airfield. The 4th Air Fleet controlled several hundred transports when the campaign began, but due to readiness issues only a portion were capable of flying supplies to the Sixth Army in late November. (Photo by Keystone/Hulton Archive/Getty Images)

The 4th Air Fleet's 9th Flak Division, commanded by Generalmajor Wolfgang Pickert, was directly assigned to support the Sixth Army as it attacked into Stalingrad. The 9th consisted of 45 batteries and 12,000 Luftwaffe personnel. As Luftwaffe Bf 109s had achieved air superiority during the first months of Operation *Blau*, the guns of the 9th were able to focus on direct support to ground operations. As throughout the war, 88mm batteries proved particularly effective against Soviet tanks. After the Soviet *Uranus* attack, the bulk of the division was encircled with the Sixth Army in the Stalingrad pocket, including 11 heavy and 19 light batteries. Other 4th Air Fleet Flak elements

Italian bombers on the Eastern Front. The Italian Expeditionary Force in Russia contained a small air support element, the ARMIR (*Armata Italiana in Russia*), but due to logistical and readiness issues the force's activity level was low. (Nik Cornish at www.Stavka.org.uk)

were dedicated to defending German airfields outside the pocket or drawn into ad hoc formations rapidly formed to assist in the ground defense of their airfields or the Chir River line.

Axis allies

The Third and Fourth Rumanian, Eighth Italian, and Second Hungarian Armies assigned to Army Group B to protect the German flanks were each supported by their own small air elements. The Rumanian *Grupparea Aeriana de Lupta* (GAL) controlled 100 aircraft of Polish, Rumanian, Italian, and German design, evenly split between fighters and bombers. The most effective were the earlier model Bf 109Es of the fighter element. Italy's ARMIR (*Armata Italiana in Russia*) brought 200 aircraft to the fight, although maintenance and spare parts shortages severely limited readiness and sortie rates. The weakest was the small Hungarian 1st Aviation Detachment (*Repuloescoport*), with only nine operational Reggiane Re 2000 Italian-designed fighters in late November.

4th Air Fleet Order of Battle, November 19, 1942

FIGHTERS
Jagdeschwader (JG) Fighter Wing 3 – Bf 109
Jagdeschwader (JG) Fighter Wing 52 – Bf 109
Heavy Fighter – Zerstörer (Destroyer)
Zerstorergeschwader (ZG) Destroyer Wing
1 – Bf 110
BOMBERS AND ATTACK
Dive bomber (Stuka)
Sturzkampfgeschwader (St.G) Stuka
Wing 1 – Ju 87
Sturzkampfgeschwader (St.G) Stuka
Wing 77 – Ju 87
Attack
Schlachtgeschwader (Sch.G) Attack Wing 1
– Bf 109, Hs 123, Hs 129
Bomber
Kampfgeschwader (KG) Bomber Wing 1 – Ju 88
Kampfgeschwader (KG) Bomber Wing 27 – He 111

Kampfgeschwader (KG) Bomber Wing
51 – He 111
Elements *Kampfgeschwader (KG)* Bomber Wing
76 – Ju 88
TRANSPORTS
Kampfgruppe zur besonderen verwendung
Special Purpose Bomber Wing 5 – He 111
(Staff) *Kampfgruppe zur besonderen verwendung*
Special Purpose Bomber Wing 1 – Ju 52
Kampfgruppe zur besonderen verwendung
Special Purpose Bomber Wing 50 – Ju 52
Kampfgruppe zur besonderen verwendung
Special Purpose Bomber Wing 102 – Ju 52
Kampfgruppe zur besonderen verwendung
Special Purpose Bomber Wing 172 – Ju 52
Kampfgruppe zur besonderen verwendung
Special Purpose Bomber Wing 900 – Ju 52

DEFENDER'S CAPABILITIES
VVS: an air force in transition

Soviet Yak-7B fighters at an airfield earlier in 1942. The 7B was a modification of the two-seat Yak-7 trainer used as a frontline fighter along with the Yak-1, La-5, and LaGG-3 during the campaign. (Photo by Sovfoto/Universal Images Group via Getty Images)

In November, 1942, the Luftwaffe was facing a Soviet opponent increasingly able to challenge it in the sky. During the early months of Operation *Blau*, the VVS was still hindered by many of the issues that crippled it in 1941: obsolete aircraft, cumbersome organization, inexperienced and poorly trained pilots, and inferior tactics. Stalin's purges had created a culture of fear and caution, and many inexperienced junior commanders were thrust into senior leadership roles. Through early 1942, Soviet aviation was organized with many of its aircraft directly controlled by ground force armies, dispersing combat power. The organization also made it extremely difficult for the VVS to integrate operations between fighters controlled by army HQs and bombers subordinate to the Front HQ. Bomber raids early in the war were rarely able to rendezvous with assigned fighter escorts, leading to heavy losses.

A new commander and new reforms

The top leadership of the VVS had experienced exceptional turmoil, with two commanders-in-chief executed during Stalin's 1938 purge, and the 1941 commander and two others who had previously served in the role shot amidst the *Barbarossa* debacle. General Pavel Zhigarev was appointed to the post on June 24, 1941, and although not executed, was transferred in April, 1942 to command Soviet air forces in the far east. In his place Stalin appointed General-Leytenant Aleksandr Novikov. Novikov had begun service during the Russian Civil War and graduated from the Frunze Military Academy in 1930 before moving to the rapidly expanding VVS in 1933. He survived Stalin's late 1930s purges of the military, being expelled from the party and air force in 1937 but readmitted the next year. He was the chief of staff of the air forces of the Leningrad Military District during the Russo–Finnish War and assumed command of the district VVS component thereafter. There, he experienced first-hand the severe disadvantages the VVS faced in battling the Luftwaffe, particularly its poor organizational structure. Novikov would rapidly launch a series of reforms that would allow the VVS to battle the Luftwaffe on more even terms.

Birth of the air armies

The VVS entered the war with a flawed organizational structure. Soviet regiments consisted of 60 aircraft, a cumbersome force to base, disperse, and control in the air, and the regiment was rapidly trimmed to just over 30 aircraft. The operational organization was also flawed, with a major portion of the aviation assigned to support each front directly attached to and controlled by the front's subordinate combined arms armies. As the armies tended to hold their own aircraft tightly, the VVS was unable to mass its combat power.

On taking command, Novikov immediately began to experiment with the formation of separate air armies (*Vozdushnya Armii*, VA) that could better control and mass aviation combat power. The ground force combined arms armies would now be left only with small composite air regiments for liaison and reconnaissance, and all the fighters, ground attack, and bomber regiments would be directly subordinate to the new VA headquarters. Three air armies – the 1st, 2nd, and 3rd – were soon formed to support the Western, Bryansk, and Kalinin Fronts, and more followed. The air armies predominantly contained "pure" fighter, ground attack, and bomber divisions and regiments, usually with each division controlling one type of aircraft rather than the less efficient mixed-type units previously used.

Aleksander Novikov, commander of the Soviet Air Force from April, 1942 through the end of the war. One of the great Eastern Front commanders, Novikov launched organizational and tactical reforms that allowed the VVS to ultimately defeat the Luftwaffe and support Red Army offensives from Stalingrad to Berlin. (Wikimedia-PD)

Formation of Soviet Air Armies (VAs)	
Date	Air Armies formed
May, 1942	1, 2,* 3, 4, 8*
June, 1942	5, 6
July, 1942	14, 15
August, 1942	16*
November, 1942	7, 13, 17*
*engaged in the Stalingrad campaign	

Each VA normally was assigned to support a front, but they could be shifted between fronts or assigned different tasks rapidly. During the Stalingrad fighting, the 2nd, 8th, 16th, and 17th VAs were engaged against the Luftwaffe's 4th Air Fleet. Air armies were to consist of 900 to 1,000 combat and support aircraft during 1942–43, although during the November, 1942–February, 1943 fighting the air armies around Stalingrad often were operating with 300–500 combat aircraft each. Backing the air armies were additional reserve air corps held directly under the Stavka and available to reinforce key sectors. By the end of 1942, 13 of these reserve corps had been formed (four fighter, three ground attack, three bomber, and three composite), and nine had been sent to the front. The reserve air corps had 120–270 aircraft at the time, and later in the war, almost as many aircraft were held in these reserve corps as were in the frontline air armies.

Novikov was able to find capable officers to lead his new air armies. General-Mayor Timofey Khryukin was 32 years old when he took over the newly formed 8th Air Army, which would play a critical role in the Stalingrad campaign. He had already been made a Hero of the Soviet Union a year after leading a volunteer force of bombers to support China's defensive campaign against Japan in 1938. He commanded the aviation of the 14th Army during the 1939–40 war with Finland, and then watched as his 64th Composite Air Division, assigned directly to the 12th Army, was destroyed during the early weeks of Operation *Barbarossa*. Sent north, Khryukin organized the defense of the Kirov railway, a vital link that allowed lend-lease supplies to be shipped from Murmansk to the south. Khryukin adeptly used the few resources available, organizing a network of airfields, radio control stations, and light beacons to support night operations. Khryukin was called to the south as the heavily attrited VVS elements were being reorganized into the new air army structure.

When the war began, the Soviets organized their aviation so that a portion of the aircraft assigned to support a front were directly subordinated to the front's armies. The first diagram on p. 29 shows the Kiev Front on June 22, 1941 – fully 59 percent of the aircraft supporting the front were actually controlled at the army level. The Soviets found that this organization dissipated their aviation power, as the armies were reluctant to release their assigned aviation assets. Air force commander Novikov instituted a new approach in early 1942, with all the aviation supporting a front centralized into a single air army organization. The second chart on p. 29 reflects the organization of the 8th Air Army on November 19, 1942, when it was assigned to support the Stalingrad Front for Operation *Uranus*. The new structure allowed the VVS to mass its aviation power when supporting front operations and more easily move air armies between fronts if required.

Novikov searched for younger, capable VVS officers to lead the new air armies organized in 1942. The 8th Air Army was ably led throughout the campaign by General Timofey Khryukin. (Wikimedia-PD)

The USSR's bomber force, DBA, had already undergone a reorganization before Novikov took command. The bombers had been used as a strike force directly commanded by VVS headquarters during the first months of the war and as a result were often ordered to conduct repeated daylight raids, resulting in massive losses. On March 5, the bombers were reorganized into a new Long-Range Aviation (ADD) command, directly controlled by the Stakva and reserved primarily for night operations or occasional critical daylight tasks.

Improving tactics

VVS operations were hindered by poor tactics in addition to cumbersome organization. Like other air forces of the early-war era such as the RAF, the VVS had entered the war employing the three-plane "vic," called a "*Katte*" by the Soviets. The formation was a legacy of the early days of air combat, when aircraft lacking radios would fly behind a flight leader and operate in response to his signals, either by hand or by wagging wings. Flying in the three-plane formation, Soviet pilots had to concentrate more on their leader and holding formation than watching for the enemy and were vulnerable to slashing attacks from above and behind by Bf 109s using their flexible *Rotte* and *Schwarm* tactics. The

Kiev Front organization on June 22, 1941

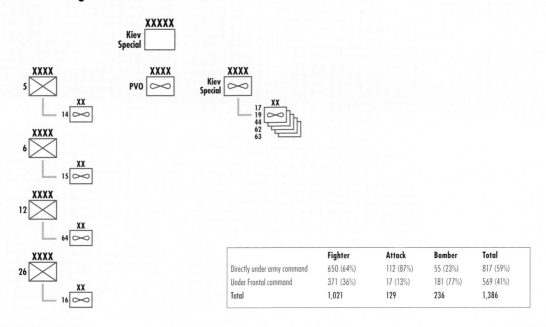

	Fighter	Attack	Bomber	Total
Directly under army command	650 (64%)	112 (87%)	55 (23%)	817 (59%)
Under Frontal command	371 (36%)	17 (13%)	181 (77%)	569 (41%)
Total	1,021	129	236	1,386

8th Air Army organization on November 19, 1942, Stalingrad

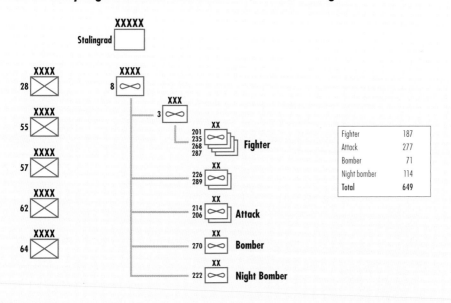

Fighter	187
Attack	277
Bomber	71
Night bomber	114
Total	649

Soviet pilots preparing for flight operations. The most critical VVS shortfall in the first years of the war was pilot training, as heavy losses drove the Soviets to send aircrew to the front with only a few hours in the air. (Courtesy of the Central Museum of the Armed Forces, Moscow, via Stavka)

early use in the war of the "taran" tactic – ramming a German plane – reflected both Soviet self-sacrifice and desperation in the face of superior German aircrew, aircraft, and tactics. By early 1942, Novikov and VVS leadership recognized the shortcomings of the *Katte* and were implementing the German finger-four plane formation, termed "*para-zveno*" in the VVS. More and more Soviet aircraft were now being equipped with full radio sets, although during the Stalingrad fighting some aircraft still had only receivers and not transmitters.

Training challenges

Pilot and aircrew training remained a major weakness that Novikov struggled to improve in 1942. Stalin demanded that frontline units have high numbers of pilots and aircraft, and to keep numbers up pilots and aircrew were sent to the front with very limited training. At times pilots flew their first mission with as few as eight hours of training in the aircraft they flew into combat. Luftwaffe training programs at the time aimed at over 300 hours, and the veterans in the ranks had performed hundreds of combat sorties. Soviet training focused on takeoff, landings, and some formation flying, with little or no instruction in combat tactics. These pilots were dubbed "takeoff and landing" by more experienced VVS airmen, and they rarely lasted longer than a few missions. Although Novikov and the high command were trying to implement improved tactics such as the use of the two- and four-plane *para-zveno* formation, use of the vertical in combat, and ambush from higher altitudes, it was difficult for the green pilots to employ these. Many VVS aircrew were intimidated by their German opponents, reluctant to engage, and often scattered when attacked, making themselves more vulnerable to pursuing German fighters. Fortunately for the VVS, Novikov ordered daytime operations be limited in the weeks prior to Operation *Uranus* to enable his forces to regroup, allowing for some combat training for Soviet airmen in the new tactics.

The fighters

The quality of VVS aircraft was improving in 1942. Soviet airmen had begun the war mostly equipped with aircraft clearly outclassed by their German opponents. Polikarpov's

I-16, a stubby monoplane, and his I-153 biplane were maneuverable – the I-16's speed and performance was comparable to that of the Hawker Hurricane – but were unable to compete with the speedier Bf 109s and their veteran pilots. These Soviet fighters were destroyed at their airfields or shot down in large numbers during *Barbarossa*, and the first modern designs to reach the front proved disappointing. The new MiG-3 fighter was designed as a high-altitude interceptor but was completely outclassed in the low-to-medium altitude dogfights that characterized Eastern Front air combat. As it used the same engine as the critical Il-2 Shturmovik, the MiG-3 was soon phased out of production. The new LaGG-3 fighter was rugged, but underpowered, overweight, and sluggish, and as it was constructed largely of wood was dubbed the *Lakirovanny Garantirovanny Grob* or "Varnished Guaranteed Coffin" by Soviet pilots. The VVS began to receive a lightened version of the LaGG-3 later in 1941 that had improved maneuverability. In November, 1942, these aircraft were also being phased out. In November, 1942 the 8th Air Army had no MiG-3s and only 20 LaGG-3s operated by three of its fighter regiments.

By late 1942, more capable fighters had entered the force in significant numbers. Semyon Lavochkin, one of the designers of the LaGG-3, mounted the powerful 1700hp Shvetsov N-82A radial engine in the LaGG-3 airframe, creating the much superior La-5 fighter. La-5 takeoffs and landings were tricky, but it proved competitive with the Bf 109s in medium- and

Soviet Yak fighters. Increased use of transmitter/receiver radios and VVS adoption of two- and four-ship tactics allowed the VVS fighter force to compete with the Bf 109s during the Stalingrad campaign. (Courtesy of the Central Museum of the Armed Forces, Moscow, via Stavka)

low-altitude combat. After the conclusion of the Stalingrad Campaign, in 1943 the upgraded La-5FN version would finally give the VVS a fighter that could fully master the Bf 109. Three 8th VA fighter regiments were flying a total of 47 La-5s at the start of the *Uranus* offensive. Ten 8th Air Army regiments were equipped with 106 Yak-1s, the other Soviet fighter design able to compete with German fighters. The Yak-1 was superior in performance to the Allies' Hurricane and P-40 fighters, and had good speed, maneuverability, and armament. Like much Soviet military equipment, it was easy to maintain and rugged. Early Yak-1s could outclass Bf 109Es but struggled to match the improved engine power and speed in the F and G models fielded in 1942. Three 8th VA regiments flew 18 of the Yak-7B variant of the Yak -1, originally a two-seat trainer converted into a fighter.

Bombers and ground attack (*Shturmovik*)

Literally in a class by itself was Sergey Ilyushin's famed Il-2 Shturmovik, an aircraft with no foreign counterpart in 1942. The pilot and engine of the Il-2 were encased in armor, giving the aircraft the ability for sustained low-level ground attack operations even when engaging heavily defended targets. The Il-2 had machine guns, cannon, and could deliver bombs and rockets. Its main weakness was the lack of rear defense, remedied as Il-2s with a rearward-facing gunner position began to join the force in late 1942. The 8th Air Army had 13 regiments equipped with 238 Il-2s in November 1942, and Novikov had a total force of 575 Shturmoviks – an unprecedented number – available to support this winter offensive.

Although pioneers of long-range strategic bombing in the interwar years, the Soviets were almost completely relying on twin-engine bombers in 1942. Their SB-2s and SB-3s were largely assigned to Long-Range Aviation and operating at night. The Petlyakov Pe-2 light bomber, however, was assigned to the air armies and capable of day horizonal and dive-bombing as well as reconnaissance tasks. It was fast, and within its class superior to the British Blenheim and roughly comparable to the Ju 88, although with a smaller bomb-carrying capacity. The 8th VA had one regiment with ten SB and four Il-4 bombers, one with obsolete Su-2s, and four regiments with a total of 41 Pe-2s.

Lend-lease aircraft

The Allies had dispatched a number of western aircraft to the USSR as part of its lend-lease program, including P-40 Tomahawk and Hurricane fighters, roughly comparable in capabilities to the Soviet fighter designs of the era. The fighters participated in the Stalingrad battles in relatively limited numbers, but several bomber divisions were equipped with the capable Douglas A-20B Boston three-seat light bomber, known as the B-3 in Soviet service, and Bostons played a major role in raids on German airfields supporting the airlift.

Reconnaissance, support, and night bombers

Unlike the Luftwaffe, the VVS lacked a dedicated, effective reconnaissance aircraft in 1942, and other types such as Pe-2 light bombers had to be used to fill the gap. Six thousand R-5 biplanes had been produced in the 1930s for reconnaissance but were obsolete and unable to operate over the front, and instead were used as utility aircraft. Forty thousand of the famous U-2 biplanes were built as training aircraft but used at the front in a wide variety of roles, including artillery spotting and air ambulance, and as a night bomber. U-2 units including the famous all-female "Night Witches" would fly U-2s at night, and while they lacked adequate bombing and navigation equipment to hit targets accurately, they continually harassed the Germans and deprived them of sleep. U-2s, also designated Po-2s to honor the designer Polikarpov, were difficult for Bf 109s to engage given their slow speed, and despite wide-scale usage had the lowest loss rate of any Soviet aircraft during the war. The 8th Air Army had seven night light bomber aviation regiments with 110 U-2s and nine R-5s.

Improvements for Stalingrad

Stalin often dispatched senior commanders to oversee and coordinate operations by multiple fronts, and in similar fashion VVS commander-in-chief Novikov arrived

VVS air armies typically controlled divisions equipped with the excellent Pe-2 light bomber, roughly comparable to the German Ju-88 and British Mosquito. The Pe-2 served throughout the war, and was capable of reconnaissance, dive-bombing, and level bombing. (Nik Cornish at www.Stavka.org.uk)

in Stalingrad in August to serve as the aviation representative of the Supreme High Command to coordinate air operations. Novikov and a small staff would continue in the role throughout the Stalingrad campaign. He ensured that the air armies supporting the *Uranus* attack had a high portion of the most modern aircraft, and by November three-fourths of all aircraft and 97 percent of the fighters were of modern design. Of the 16th Air Army's 125 fighters, only nine were outdated types. Novikov ordered the construction of a large number of airfields east of the Volga and north of the Don to support the operations, including dummy bases. Most of the bases, however, had primitive infrastructure with personnel relegated to sleeping in dugouts or tents. Supplies were short, including fuel, ammunition, and spare parts. Soviet aircraft were rugged, however, and aided by the reduction of operations before Operation *Uranus,* the VVS was able to maintain readiness rates of over 70 percent.

Novikov had experimented with ground radio control while VVS commander at Leningrad and directed the 16th Air Army to implement such a system at Stalingrad on a larger scale. Radio control stations were established 1–2 miles behind the front lines and separated from each other by 8km. Manned by commanders and deputy commanders called up from reserve squadrons, the stations maintained communications with air army headquarters and regiments at their airfields while monitoring friendly and enemy air operations. The guidance net included both command and information posts and was used to guide fighters to intercept enemy aircraft and eventually ground attack aircraft to their targets.

To help offset the skills of the veteran Luftwaffe pilots, 8th Air Army commander Khryukin decided to form a special "ace regiment." The 9th Guards Independent Fighter Regiment had already proven itself and was known as "the regiment of the heroes of the Soviet Union," and Khryukin identified a series of successful VVS pilots and sent them to the 9th. The regiment traded in its LaGG-3s for more capable Yak-1s equipped with the best available radio equipment. Khryukin held the unit out of combat for several weeks, and it engaged in intensive training in the *para-zveno* tactics. When sent into battle on December 11, the unit shot down four Ju 52s in its first engagement and became one of the top-scoring VVS units during the campaign.

VVS Order of Battle, November 19, 1942

8TH AIR ARMY
Two Composite Air Corps
214th Attack Aviation Division
201st Fighter Aviation Division
236th Fighter Aviation Division
268th Fighter Aviation Division
287th Fighter Aviation Division
226th Composite Air Division
206th Attack Aviation Division
289th Composite Aviation Division
270th Bomber Aviation Division
272nd Night Bomber Aviation Division
8th Reconnaissance Aviation Regiment
16TH AIR ARMY
220nd Fighter Aviation Division
283rd Fighter Aviation Division
228th Attack Aviation Division

291st Attack Aviation Division
271st Night Aviation Division
17TH AIR ARMY
282nd Fighter Aviation Division
221st Bomber Aviation Division
262nd Night Bomber Aviation Division
208th Attack Aviation Division
637th Attack Aviation Division
1st Composite Air Corps
288th Fighter Aviation Division
267th Attack Aviation Division
102ND AIR DEFENSE (PVO) DIVISION
572nd Fighter Regiment
629th Fighter Regiment
652nd Fighter Regiment
788th Fighter Regiment

CAMPAIGN OBJECTIVES
Keystone on the Volga

Hitler's primary goal in November was to retain the admittedly limited gains the Wehrmacht had achieved in its summer 1942 offensive. The immediate strategic issue after November 23, however, was the fate of Paulus' encircled Sixth Army at Stalingrad, and its ultimate destruction made Hitler's decision to have it stand fast one of the most controversial of the war. The Luftwaffe's ability to supply the pocket was intertwined with the "stand fast" order, yet this aspect of the decision process has typically only been covered briefly in most accounts of the campaign, with blame being assigned almost solely to Luftwaffe commander-in-chief Reichsmarschall Hermann Göring. The actual decision-making process was more complex and featured additional players.

When the first reports of the *Uranus* offensive came to Hitler's attention on November 19,¸ he was taking a brief respite from his normal headquarters at his Berghof retreat in Berchtesgaden. The Führer was already dealing with a wide variety of crises, including the defeat of the Africa Korps at El Alamein, the Allied *Torch* landings in French North Africa, the occupation of Vichy France, and the reinforcement of Tunisia. Hitler ordered Paulus to form a 360-degree defense when the Sixth Army was threatened with encirclement the next day, and it soon became clear that he was resolved that Stalingrad be held at all costs, a decision in line with his instincts throughout the war. Hitler demanded that German forces stand fast whenever they were forced on the defensive and forbade even tactical withdrawals, an approach that stabilized the front during the winter of 1941–42 but would prove disastrous afterwards. That Stalingrad bore Stalin's name, had been so costly to attack, and had been made a feature of Hitler's triumphal speeches during the fall all played a role in increasing the Führer's resolve. As the Soviets continued their offensive during the winter and began to threaten to destroy the entire German military position in the southern USSR, cold military calculation further dictated that the Sixth Army hold out to the last to tie down as many Red Army units as possible.

Hitler and his senior officers at an early 1943 Army Group South planning session. Richthofen is on the far right, and Manstein on the far left. Unfortunately for the German war effort, the decision to maintain the Sixth Army by air in November, 1942 was made with all the key decision makers scattered, and Richthofen was unable to reach Hitler with his doubts about the plan. (Photo by ullstein bild/ullstein bild via Getty Images)

The two key Luftwaffe players in the decision to supply the Sixth Army by air were the commander-in-chief Göring, and to his left in the photo, Chief of Staff Hans Jeschonnek. Jeschonnek made the first estimate to Hitler that the airlift was practicable and lacked the force of character to make the Führer understand his revised calculations. Göring arrived relatively late in the decision-making process, but to shore up his standing with Hitler claimed the Luftwaffe could do the job. (Narodowe Archiwum Cyfrowe/Public Domain)

Hitler ordered Manstein to take command of a new Army Group Don that would assemble arriving reinforcements and launch a relief operation. Four panzer and six infantry divisions would be allocated, although most of the reinforcements would only arrive in early December at the earliest. With the recent successful aerial supply of the Demyansk pocket, thoughts at the Berghof turned to the potential for the Luftwaffe to sustain Stalingrad until it could be relieved. Göring was absent at his Karinhall estate, presiding over a conference on Axis oil supplies, but Luftwaffe chief of staff Hans Jeschonnek was called to Berchtesgaden on November 20. The Führer typically demanded immediate answers to his questions, and Jeschonnek gave Hitler an on-the-spot assessment that the resupply of the Sixth Army should be possible for a limited period given adequate numbers of aircraft and secure airfields. Jeschonnek soon revised his estimate after a more considered analysis, and after hearing from Richthofen and the commanders at the front. The initial quick calculations proved to be flawed, based on 1,000kg and 750kg supply containers being able to carry those amounts. It was soon discovered, however, that these measurements derived from the size of the bombs they replaced, and they only held about two-thirds of those amounts. Hitler, however, had been given the answer he wanted and Jeschonnek lacked the force of personality to get him to acknowledge the revised estimate.

The Luftwaffe commanders at the scene had no hesitation and voiced their opposition to relying on an airlift to maintain the Sixth Army in place from the first. Richthofen and Fiebig asserted to Jeschonnek, Göring, and Paulus that a successful airlift was impossible given the size of the Sixth Army – almost three times that of the two corps at Demyansk – and problems with basing and the looming winter weather. They also made a convert of the OKH (Army) chief of staff, Kurt Zeitzler. General Wolfgang Pickert, commander of the 9th Flak Division supporting the Sixth Army, similarly told the Sixth Army chief of staff, General Arthur Schmidt, that an airlift was impossible and urged a breakout, offering to support the operation with manhandled 20mm anti-aircraft guns to help clear the way. Paulus' corps commanders, led by the XI's Walther von Seydlitz-Kurzbach, urged that the army abandon the Stalingrad position and immediately break out to rejoin German lines, but Paulus and Schmidt were worried by the army's lack of fuel and felt a breakout could lead to destruction on the open steppe. Pressured by his commanders, however, Paulus asked Hitler for freedom of action.

Hitler never gave Paulus that flexibility, and isolated at the Berghof until the 23rd neither sought nor heard the perspective of the Luftwaffe commanders at the front. Richthofen, a dedicated national socialist and aggressive commander favored by the Führer, might have had an impact with him but his attempts to make his views known never succeeded. OKH (Army) chief of staff Zeitzler was the only officer with Hitler at this point urging a breakout, and the skeleton OKW staffs led by Wilhelm Keitel, a notorious sycophant, and Alfred Jodl strongly backed Hitler's decision to hold at Stalingrad. When he finally arrived on the scene, Göring did nothing to make Hitler aware of the views of Richthofen and the commanders at the front, nor was he willing to bring Jeschonnek's revised calculations to Hitler's attention. Nervous about his standing with Hitler, Göring asserted that the Luftwaffe could do the job, later saying in private that he had no choice but to take that stand, given that Hitler "had him by the sword knot." Göring ordered that all resources be dedicated to the airlift, even his personal VIP transport plane, but rather than supervise the critical operation immediately departed in his luxuriously outfitted personal train "Asia" for an art-buying trip to Paris.

The decision process had been marred by poor communications and flawed staff processes, with Hitler, Jeschonnek, and Göring bearing primary responsibility for the result. Hitler

Göring with Luftwaffe officers. After pledging to Hitler that his air force could resupply Paulus' Sixth Army at Stalingrad, Göring departed on his luxurious personal train, "Asia," for Paris to shop for art. (Nik Cornish at www.Stavka.org.uk)

Stalin was the ultimate decision maker for Soviet military operations, often forcing his senior officers into hasty and ill-advised attacks that resulted in heavy losses. By the winter of 1942, he listened more to his senior military leaders, in particular Zhukov and Vasilevskiy, Chief of the General Staff, resulting in better-orchestrated and more successful offensive operations. (Wikimedia-PD)

almost certainly never entertained any idea of allowing a withdrawal from Stalingrad. He never sought a comprehensive analysis of the Luftwaffe's capabilities, nor did he listen to Jeschonnek when he tried to bring his corrected assessment to the Führer's attention. The perspectives of the commanders at the front never reached the Berghof, and a frustrated Richthofen vented in his diary that "we are nothing less than highly-paid non-commissioned officers." Göring arrived relatively late in the decision-making process but was ultimately responsible for the Luftwaffe's acceptance of the task. He lacked the moral courage to challenge Hitler and refused to demand or bring forward staff analyses or recommendations from Richthofen and the 4th Air Fleet commanders to question the Führer's "iron will."

There was hope that the airlift would be a temporary effort, and Manstein would soon break through and relieve the Sixth Army, but Hitler was determined that, in any case, what he now termed "Fortress Stalingrad" would have to hold out, if need be, until a spring offensive could restore the German front. Whatever the duration of the effort, the Luftwaffe's task was daunting. There would be heavy demands on the 4th Air Fleet's limited numbers of fighter and bomber aircraft, as they would need to conduct the airlift, defend the front line, support the troops in the pocket, and help the relief column once it began its attack. As to the tonnage to be flown, the Sixth Army assessed it required 750 tons of supplies a day for full capabilities, with 500 being adequate to maintain the army, and 300 tons a minimum for sustainment.

Soviet objectives

Stalin and the high command aimed at nothing less than the destruction of one or more of the German army groups inside the USSR, accompanied by the seizure of all the territory lost in 1942, if not more. In addition to the campaign in the south, winter offensives were planned against Army Group Center and to relieve the siege of Leningrad. With Paulus' forces encircled in Stalingrad, the Stavka was planning to eliminate the pocket, which they initially estimated contained around 95,000 troops, and then launch a follow-on operation named *Saturn* to seize Rostov and trap Army Group A in the Caucasus. Soviet forces would then exploit in further attacks to the west. Like the Luftwaffe, the VVS would face multiple tasks, maintaining the encirclement, supporting *Saturn* and additional offensives, soon joined by the requirement to block Luftwaffe supply flights into the pocket.

THE CAMPAIGN

The turning point on the Eastern Front

November 24–30: establishing an airlift

The Luftwaffe faced a chaotic situation after *Uranus*. The poor weather grounded reconnaissance aircraft, leaving the precise status of the front uncertain, and airfields were overcrowded with aircraft that had evacuated from forward bases. Ground personnel at these were struggling to move critical aircraft support equipment and vehicles out before Red Army tanks arrived, while ad-hoc units were formed to man trenches around the runways. Richthofen ordered the immediate evacuation of the exposed airfields, Luftwaffe command posts, and facilities between Stalingrad and the Don and recalled most of his aircraft from the Caucasus. Only two fighter groups and some reconnaissance squadrons were left to provide a measure of support to Army Group A. As the trap closed behind the Sixth Army, the 4th Air Fleet began to turn its attention to the airlift operation.

With clearing weather on the 25th, Luftwaffe reconnaissance was at last able to fly and target Soviet forces. The VIII Air Corps headquarters at Oblivskaya was under direct assault by the Soviet 5th Tank Army, and its *Schlacht* attack aircraft, Stukas, Bf 109s, and He 111s launched repeated sorties against the tanks and vulnerable cavalry, with low-flying He 111s effective but suffering losses to ground fire. The 8th Cavalry Corps reported four regimental commanders, 500 troops, and 1,500 horses lost due to the air attack. The next day, Rudel flew 17 sorties with his Stukas, and with ground-attack Hs 123s and Hs 129s, repeatedly hit Soviet artillery and tank formations. The last tank was destroyed at the edge of the airfield. In Stalingrad, the reconnaissance aircraft posted at Pitomnik airfield were able to guide Paulus as he shifted his forces to cover the entire 120-mile pocket perimeter.

Only small numbers of transports reached the Sixth Army in the first days after *Uranus*, and even after the formal start of the airlift on November 24, readiness and weather problems limited sorties – an augur of problems that would dog the entire operation. Richthofen began

Ju 86 bombers pictured in 1937. The Ju 86 was developed at the same time as the He 111 but proved inferior during the Spanish Civil War and was relegated to the training establishment after 1939. Two air groups totaling 58 Ju 86s were sent to the Stalingrad airlift. (*Flight Global/* CC-BY-SA 4.0)

Richthofen gave General Martin Fiebig and his VIII Air Corps staff control of the airlift on November 30. The staff was expert at air superiority and close support operations but lacked experience with running a large-scale airlift. (Bundesarchiv, Bild 146-1968-015-48 / CC-BY-SA 3.0 DE)

the operation with roughly 295 transports, but readiness was low, roughly 30 percent, and the aircraft were still heavily committed to bringing up supplies for the 4th Air Fleet itself. Forty-two Ju 52s were operational at Tatsinskaya on the 24th, and all reached Pitomnik, delivering 84 tons of fuel. Thirty-three flew the next day, and 35 the day after. Only 14 Ju 52s braved snowstorms to reach Pitomnik the next day, delivering 28 tons of fuel. Richthofen directed He 111s to augment the Ju 52s, and they joined the transport operation on November 29. The VVS was already in action against the transports, and 13 Ju 52s were lost during the last three days of the month, along with six He 111s lost or severely damaged. By the 30th the airlift had managed to land a total of 526 tons, only a fraction of the 2,100 theoretical total needed to meet the minimum requirement for 300 tons a day for November 24–30. Richthofen realized action was required to better organize the effort.

Setting up the airlift – the task

The encircled Sixth Army had been fighting an intense battle at the end of a long and inadequate supply line and would need rapid resupply. The single-line track connecting Rostov to Stalingrad had been cut by a destroyed bridge at the Don for most of the fall, and Paulus' troops had to transload supplies and transport them 75km by truck to its forward depots. Although the railroad had been fully extended to Stalingrad by late November, its capacity remained limited, and Paulus had prioritized the delivery of artillery ammunition to support the intense fighting for the city. The Sixth Army had never been able to accumulate an adequate stockpile of food and other supplies, and the *Uranus* offensive had overrun many of the supply depots in the Sixth Army's rear areas.

German staffs assessed the Sixth Army would require 750 tons of supplies daily to maintain its full capability. In theory, 375 daily Ju 52 sorties, each fully loaded with two tons of supplies, would meet the army's needs, although more sorties would have to be flown on days with good weather to compensate for those with poor flying conditions. The Luftwaffe had 750 Ju 52s, and even with a third assigned to the Mediterranean theater, it could theoretically have performed the task if most of the transports were operational. Ju 52 readiness on the Eastern Front averaged 30–35 percent, however, and at that rate a theoretical force of 1,050 Ju 52s would be needed. Even had they been in existence, the airfield and logistical support infrastructure at the front would have been unable to accommodate or support them. Given these limitations, the Luftwaffe and Sixth Army identified more achievable goals. Five hundred tons a day was considered adequate to support the Sixth Army and allow it to retain some combat power. The bare minimum needed for sustenance was 300 tons daily, but the army's fighting abilities would begin to deteriorate at that level. As Army Group Don was preparing a relief operation, it was hoped that the airlift would only have to supply the pocket for a few weeks. To enable the Sixth Army to have enough mobility to attack to meet the relief column, fuel supplies were the initial priority, followed by ammunition. The troops were to rely on the six days of rations on hand and then slaughtering their horses to subsist until help arrived.

The 4th Air Fleet only had limited numbers of its organic Ju 52 force available for the first supply runs into the pocket, but the transports were a welcome sight to troops in the encircled Sixth Army. Richthofen augmented the Ju 52s with He 111s used as transports, and the first landed at Pitomnik on November 29. (Nik Cornish at www.Stavka.org.uk)

Command and control

Göring assigned the airlift mission to the 4th Air Fleet; the leader of the Demyansk airlift, Oberst Fritz Morzik, was not employed or even consulted for the Stalingrad operation. Richthofen initially appointed Generalmajor Victor Caraganico, the Tatsinskaya Airfield commander, as *Luftversorgungsführer* (air supply leader) to run the airlift. Caraganico was a good airfield logistics officer but lacked experience controlling air operations and struggled for several days to get the airlift moving. Caraganico was unused to working with the fighters needed to escort the transports through Soviet defenses. Frustrated, Richthofen replaced him with Generalleutnant Martin Fiebig and the VIII Air Corps command staff on November 30. The VIII brought with it a full communications network and weather monitoring stations, but while expert in close support operations had no experience in running a large-scale airlift. As the next weeks would show, the VIII Air Corps would be unable to overcome the numerous logistical, operational, and maintenance issues that plagued the operation. With more Ju 52s arriving, Fiebig concentrated them at Tatsinskaya Airfield to simplify maintenance and support. Airfield commander Oberst Hans Förster took over command of the ten groups of Ju 52s and two groups of Ju 86s there. He 111 operations were run from Morozovsk under Oberst Ernst Kühl, commander of the He 111 55th Bomber Wing. Kühl was given the dual task of using his bombers as transports but remaining ready to conduct bombing missions to support the Chir River defenses that protected the airlift airfields.

Richthofen designated Generalmajor Pickert, the 9th Flak Division's leader, as commander of all Luftwaffe troops and operations in the pocket. Aware of Pickert's lack of seniority, Fiebig offered to send a more senior Luftwaffe officer into the pocket to supervise the airlift effort there, but Paulus refused. Pickert controlled roughly 12,000 encircled air force personnel trapped with the Sixth Army, including the division's 11 heavy and 19 light Flak batteries and assorted signals and support personnel. Pickert worked vigorously to ready and equip the primary airfield within the pocket, Pitomnik, to receive enough supplies to support 250,000 troops. Detachments of the 3rd Fighter and 2nd Stuka Wings, along with some reconnaissance aircraft, continued to operate from Pitomnik.

An He 111 bomber flying supplies to the Stalingrad pocket. The He 111s proved extremely useful to the airlift, actually flying more sorties to the Sixth Army than the Ju 52s, and more survivable due to their better speed and superior defensive armament. (Photo by Sobotta/ullstein bild via Getty Images)

Assembling the transports

The German military viewed the Ju 52 as primarily an asset for dropping airborne troops into battle when needed and lacked a large standing transport force. When needed, additional Ju 52s and crews were surged from the training establishment to form provisional units to augment the one permanent (1st) Transport Wing and then disbanded and returned to their training roles. This system had worked in 1940 and 1941, although the Ju 52 force had suffered heavy losses during the battle for Crete. The Luftwaffe used the same surge system to supply the Demyansk pocket, augmenting the limited number of Ju 52s at the front with aircraft and crews pulled from training units in the Reich.

In November, 1942, the Luftwaffe contained a total of 750 Ju 52s, with a third supporting operations in Tunisia. Given the size of the force to be supplied at Stalingrad, the Luftwaffe went to extraordinary lengths to obtain additional transports for the airlift. The training establishment was stripped of aircraft and instructor pilots, along with some Ju 52s pulled from support to Mediterranean operations. Lufthansa airliners and other government couriers, VIP transport, and postal service Ju 52s were ruthlessly searched out and sent to augment the airlift. All these aircraft needed to be prepared and conditioned for winter flying, and the civilian ones equipped for military operations. The Luftwaffe established conversion workshops at Kirovograd and Zaporozhnye in Ukraine to prepare the transports but struggled to handle the large numbers of incoming Ju 52s, many of which were older and well used. Pressure from above to rapidly increase the numbers of transports at the front led to many inadequately prepared Ju 52s being rushed forward. One estimate assessed that only about 40 percent of the aircraft were fully prepared to operate in the Russian winter, with many lacking the necessary defensive armament, radios, and direction-finding equipment, or insulation. Some Lufthansa Ju 52s arrived at Tatsinskaya with passenger seats still in the cargo area that needed to be removed, much to the disgust of the ground crews. At Morozovsk, Oberst Kühl complained about the serviceability of the He 111s of the 20th Wing, a unit filled out with older airframes taken from depot storage. As a result, both forward airfields rapidly became crowded with non-operational transports.

German transport Order of Battle, early December				
Units	Aircraft type	Comments	Total number December 15	Total number January 15
9, 50, 102, 105, 172, 500, 700, 900 Special Duty Bomber Groups (Kampfgeschwader zu besonderen Verwendung), 1 and 2 Gp/1st Special Duty Bomber Wing (I/KG.z.b.V, II/KG.z.b.V)	Ju 52s	Many from training establishment (Ju 52s used as multi-engine trainers)	241	317
5 and 20 Special Duty Bomber Groups (Kampfgruppen), 27 and 55 Bomber Wings (Kampfgeschwader), 1st Group, 100 Bomber Wing (I/100 KG), and 3rd Group, 4 Bomber Wing (III/4 KG)	He 111s	5 and 20 He 111 units specializing in transport missions; others bomber units used in transport role	132	222
21 and 22 Special Duty Bomber Groups (Kampfgruppen)	Ju 86s	Bombers used as trainers, assigned to operate as transports	67	0
50 Bomber Wing (Kampfgeschwader)	He 177	Developmental long-range bomber, very troubled; joined airlift January, 1943	0	28 He 177
200 Special Duty Bomber Group (Kampfgruppe)	Fw 200, Ju 290	Ad hoc unit of maritime reconnaissance Condors and Ju 90, 290 airliners; joined airlift January, 1943	0	19 Fw 200 2 Ju 290

The Ju 52 was the primary German transport aircraft of World War II. It was used as a bomber with the Condor Legion during the Spanish Civil War, but by 1939 was dedicated to dropping paratroopers, delivering supplies, and serving as a trainer. Known as "Auntie Tu" or "Iron Annie," the aircraft was a capable transport with a wide side door for loading and able to deliver two tons of supplies on each sortie. The Ju 52 carried only two machine guns for defense, however, and its cruising speed of 130mph made it difficult for speedy Bf 109s to escort and vulnerable to Soviet fighters and even Il-2 Shturmoviks. To augment the Ju 52s, additional He 111 bombers were converted to a transport role. The bombers could carry 1.1 tons of supplies, although the need to use the bomb bay doors for supply operations complicated loading and unloading. The He 111s proved better able to fly, maneuver, and defend themselves with their stronger defensive armament. Soviet pilots often sought out the Ju 52s rather than attack the more dangerous He 111s. The airlift was burdened with less useful aircraft. The Ju 86 bomber had been developed in the 1930s but, as it was inferior to the He 111, was used as a trainer. Bomber Groups 21 and 22 were drawn from the training schools and arrived at Tatsinskaya with their obsolete Ju 86 bombers in early December. The aircraft had serviceability issues, a limited cargo capacity, and suffered heavy losses. The 16 Ju 86s that successfully escaped the Soviet tank attack on Tatsinskaya Airfield on December 24 were sent back to the Reich. DFS 230 and Go 244 freight gliders had been used during the Demyansk airlift to deliver supplies, but after consideration the Luftwaffe rejected their use at Stalingrad as they would require special preparations at the airfields and would only be usable in good weather. The transport force was slow to gather, as some Ju 52s had to fly 1,000 miles or more just to reach the preparation centers, but ultimately ten groups of Ju 52s, seven groups of He 111s, and two groups of Ju 86s had gathered for the airlift, amounting to 369 transports on December 3, although only 30–50 percent were operational on any given day. Small numbers of Italian Fiat BR.20M and Rumanian Ju 52s also flew in the airlift.

German troops consume hot rations during winter conditions. The Sixth Army's poor logistical state even before the encirclement meant that food reserves were limited, and the daily rations were reduced almost immediately. It was hoped that the Sixth Army could eat its small stockpiles, emergency rations, and slaughter its horses to hold out until relieved. (Nik Cornish at www.Stavka.org.uk)

The supplies

On November 23, the Army Group Don staff assessed that the Sixth Army needed 100 tons of ammunition a day for normal operations and 75 tons of fuel to allow the panzer divisions and anti-aircraft units to perform defensive tasks. More would be required to build adequate reserves for a breakout operation or heavier defensive fighting. As for rations, troops engaged in heavy defensive operations in winter weather need at least 2,500 calories a day, and supplying 250,000 soldiers at this level would require 282 tons. Paulus' headquarters reported that it had six days of rations on hand and anticipating difficulties with aerial resupply reduced the army's daily rations to 1,500 calories a day on November 26 and 1,000 on December 8. The Sixth Army had sent all but 23,000 of its 90,000 horses west for the winter prior to the *Uranus* attack, and slaughtering the remaining horses for food would reduce the full ration requirement to 255 tons a day as long as the meat lasted. Given the hope for a rapid relief of the pocket and the potential for the Sixth Army to launch some sort of breakout to meet the relief force, the initial transport flights predominantly flew in fuel, some ammunition, and very few rations.

The quality of some supplies sent to the Sixth Army turned out to be substandard as the quartermasters scrambled to fill the transports. Concentrated foods such as those issued to U-boat crews would have been ideal, as the troops had plenty of water to hydrate them, but most of the rations sent were frozen lumps of fresh meat and vegetables, with three-quarters of the weight of the rations wasted when thawed. Frozen rye bread was also dispatched while stocks of wheat flour and butter remained untouched at Rostov due to bureaucratic inefficiency and administrative red tape. Cumbersome Christmas trees sent in December as a morale-raising measure also took up precious cargo space. When he arrived in mid-January with a mandate from Hitler to improve the airlift, Generalfeldmarschall Erhard Milch demanded improvements in the quality of supplies after spot-checks revealed some crates only contained fishmeal. There were also reports of useless supplies such as condoms and mosquito repellant being flown in, although Pickert stated in his post-war account that this was a minor issue. One type of supply that generated no complaints was mail to and from the troops. About two tons of mail was flown in daily, amounting to a total of 73 tons by December 31. Each outgoing flight also carried out mail along with wounded, and 15 tons and 18,410 wounded had left Pitomnik by the same date.

The airfields and logistics, late November, 1942

Well-equipped, supplied, and secure airfields were critical to the success of the airlift. Tatsinskaya and Morozovsk – known in Luftwaffe slang as "Tazi" and "Moro" – were the primary bases used from November to December. Tatsinskaya was 160 miles from Stalingrad, Morozovsk 140 miles, allowing for 50–90 minute transport flight times. Even allowing time for loading, unloading, and servicing, more than one sortie per day should have been possible, but due to the limited capabilities of the ground staffs most operational transports flew only one sortie a day at most. Both airfields had been primarily used by the Rumanian air element before *Uranus*, with Morozovsk also used to support German He 111 operations. The limited hangars and parking facilities at the two fields were soon overwhelmed by several hundred additional aircraft arriving to support the airlift. Morozovsk had hangars and taxiways but suffered the loss of munitions and fuel destroyed by panicking Rumanian units on November 20. Tatsinskaya similarly had several hangars, workshops, and huts to house base personnel, but even before the arrival of the airlift reinforcements aircrews had complained that ground support was inadequate. After *Uranus*, Tatsinskaya was crowded with ten air groups of Ju 52s and two of Ju 86s, and Morozovsk with seven He 111 groups, and both airfields hosted various reconnaissance and dive-bomber aircraft displaced from the forward fields overrun by the Soviet offensive and still required to support the defense of the Chir line.

Maintenance personnel and spare parts were also inadequate. One Airfield Servicing Company was needed to support each air group, and the six companies at Tatsinskaya and the four at Morozovsk were unable to cope with the numbers of transports and other aircraft at their respective fields. Ground support staffs were undermanned as personnel and support equipment had been lost during the hasty evacuation of forward bases, and others were in ad hoc ground units defending the airfields and Chir front. Some of the Ju 52s rushed to augment the airlift were well-used older models, as were many of the bombers used as transports, and shortages of spare parts rapidly became a problem. Both bases stocked some He 111 supplies, as they had been supporting bomber operations during the fall, but the nearest Ju 52 spare parts were held at Stalino. With all available transports being used to fly to the pocket, the 4th Air Fleet could no longer use Ju 52s to fly supplies up to its forward fields as it had during the autumn, and more and more aircraft became unserviceable. Large numbers of transports throughout the airlift assigned to the 4th Air Fleet were undergoing repairs in rear-area maintenance facilities and not available at the forward fields.

Ju 52s at an airfield in the USSR with a measure of infrastructure. Tatsinskaya and Morozovsk had some hangars and workshops but were soon overwhelmed by the large numbers of transports arriving to support the airlift, and almost all servicing and loading had to be performed in the freezing winter weather. (Nik Cornish at www.Stavka.org.uk)

Airlift operations and tactics, November 24–December 11, 1942

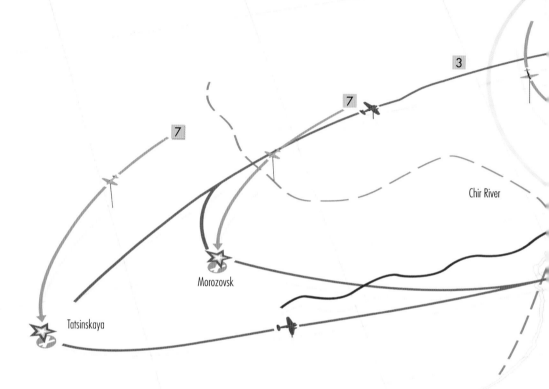

3

7

7

Chir River

Morozovsk

Tatsinskaya

EVENTS

1. The Luftwaffe began daylight air transport operations in clear weather by gathering groups of five to ten or more transports and providing fighter escort. The slow cruising speed of Ju 52s made it difficult for the Bf 109s to remain with them, and they weaved or climbed and dived above the transports to maintain station. This used up fuel and meant that the Bf 109s could not escort the transports all the way to Pitomnik. German transport crews tended to fly at lower levels, trusting in low clouds or fog or their camouflage to avoid Soviet fighters, and some felt the Bf 109s only served to alert the VVS to their presence.

2. Transports typically had to vary their routes to the pocket to avoid the massed Soviet anti-aircraft guns on the most obvious flight paths. Southern approaches were often used. The longer routes used more fuel and decreased the amount of supplies that could be transported.

3. Ju 52s with experienced crews and He 111s often flew to the pocket at low altitude, without fighter escort, flying singly or in small groups. The transports exploited low clouds or fog or flew at night.

The transports would pop up to 3,000 ft or so over the front line and when transiting the perimeter of the pocket to try to avoid ground fire.

4. VVS Commander-in-Chief Novikov established an air blockade system in early December to halt German air supply flights. Soviet units were assigned specific sectors to patrol, gaining familiarity with the local conditions. A Soviet radio-control network monitored flight operations and vectored fighters onto the transports. The VVS assigned its most experienced pilots to serve as *otoniki* or "free hunters" to patrol the zone and engage when vectored or when they identified targets of opportunity. The interceptors inflicted significant losses on the transports in the first weeks of December.

5. The air blockade system included a zone of 5–10 miles reserved for Soviet 37 and 85mm anti-aircraft guns and machine guns used in an AA role. The Luftwaffe lacked adequate resources to strike the Soviet AAA positions.

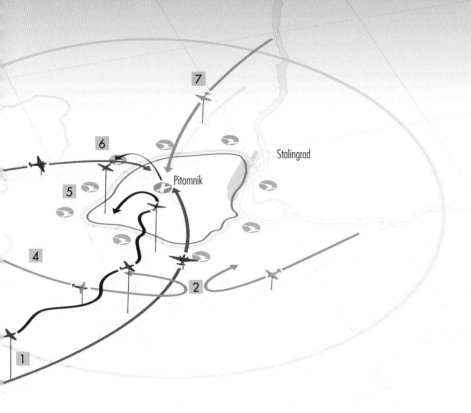

7

6

Stalingrad

Pitomnik

5

4

2

1

EVENTS

6. The detachment of Bf 109s at Pitomnik attempted to provide escort for incoming transports, but the Luftwaffe never established an effective radio net to facilitate effective linkups, and the fighters and transports often missed one another in foggy or cloudy conditions. The fighters were also typically diverted by the need to defend the Stalingrad perimeter or Pitomnik itself.

7. The Soviet air blockade included an offensive component, and VVS bombers and fighter bombers frequently raided Tatsinskaya and Morozovsk and, within the pocket, Pitomnik.

Neither of the bases was adequately prepared for operations during the harsh Russian winter, and the transports had to be serviced, fueled, and loaded in the open. With many days of below-zero temperatures, icing, fog, and blizzards, the ground support crews struggled to ready enough aircraft and clear runways of snowdrifts with pick and shovel. Ground personnel suffered from frostbite, illness, and exhaustion, and the time to "turn around" an aircraft and ready it for flight doubled from two to four hours as the weather worsened. Shortages of the *Warmewagen* vehicles used to warm and start aircraft engines was another complication. A post-airlift assessment noted that only 20 percent of the *Warmewagens* needed for the number of transports were available, leading to long delays in beginning operations each day. Conditions would be even worse when the airlift was driven to even more poorly equipped bases in January, and equipment, including the *Warmewagens*, was not evacuated to the new fields.

Pitomnik was the primary airfield in the pocket able to receive supply flights, and Pickert ensured it was equipped with signals facilities, *X-Gerät* and *Y-Gerät* radio homing beacons, and lights and a flare path to assist with night and low-visibility operations. Pickert and his 9th Flak Division staff established teams, equipment, and procedures to rapidly unload and service arriving transports and distribute the supplies to the Sixth Army. Aircraft wrecks on the airfield from crashes and VVS air raids needed to be constantly cleared as the siege continued. Stalingrad–Basargino was used to a limited extent as an overflow field but lacked Pitomnik's infrastructure. The other major airfield available in the pocket was Gumrak, and the Luftwaffe urged that it be prepared and used to receive transports or at least be ready if Pitomnik was unusable, but the Sixth Army refused, worried that work on the field would attract Soviet attention to their nearby HQ.

Weather and flight operations

Ideally, an airlift would consist of a constant stream of transports landing throughout the day, allowing rapid unloading and turn-around at several receiving airfields, but the weather and threat of Soviet interception prevented such an ideal operations tempo. The Pitomnik ground crews thus often faced hours of inactivity and then the arrival of numbers of incoming aircraft that overwhelmed their capability to handle rapidly. Richthofen and Fiebig had warned from the first that poor weather would make a successful airlift impossible. The mean winter temperature in Stalingrad was 17.9 degrees Fahrenheit, two degrees colder than the temperature in Leningrad far to the north. Snowfall was frequent, and the wind blew it into huge drifts on the open steppe. Roads, taxiways, and runways had to be constantly plowed, with hand tools if snowplows were not available. Difficulties starting the aircraft in the cold winter weather led to long morning delays and transports taking off whenever they could be started. In the air, transports were lost or forced to abort due to icing, snow squalls, and poor visibility.

In clear weather, to protect against Soviet fighters, the Luftwaffe

Ground support equipment at a German airfield. The Luftwaffe was unable to keep the needed number of its transports ready to fly due to shortages of maintenance personnel and equipment compounded by the difficulties of working on the aircraft during the severe winter conditions. (Nik Cornish at www.Stavka.org.uk)

The Luftwaffe initially attempted to provide escorts for groups of transports but was forced to abandon daylight Ju 52 flight operations in clear weather in mid-December due to Soviet fighters and difficulties with Bf 109 escort operations. (Nik Cornish at www.Stavka.org.uk)

gathered transports into groups of at least five, and ideally of squadron strength of ten or more, and defended them with fighter escorts. The Bf 109s had trouble escorting the slow Ju 52s. The Bf 109s' stalling speed meant that the fighters had to weave or climb and dive to remain with the Ju 52s, burning up fuel and preventing the fighters from providing escort all the way to Pitomnik. Two 52nd Fighter Wing Bf 109s were lost when they ran out of fuel trying to escort Ju 52s all the way in on one of the first missions on November 28. The transports typically also had to fly circuitous routes to Pitomnik to try to avoid concentrations of Soviet anti-aircraft guns, further worsening the Bf 109s' fuel problem. The Luftwaffe had fighter drop tanks, but red tape and bureaucratic slowness prevented their arrival until late January. Many Ju 52s preferred to fly at low altitudes to avoid detection, using their camouflage to blend in with the ground or seeking cover in low clouds or haze, and some transport pilots felt that the weaving Bf 109 fighter escorts 3,000–10,000 feet overhead only served to draw the attention of Soviet interceptors. Many of the more capable pilots preferred to try to reach the pocket without escorts, hugging the ground and only popping up to avoid small arms fire when over the front.

Fiebig's limited fighter force – around 50 Bf 109s at the start of *Uranus*, and around 90 in late November – were in any case hard pressed to provide adequate escorts for the transports. The fighters were needed to cover their own airfields from enemy raids and help defend the weak Chir line, which was under continual Soviet attack, leaving about 40 Bf 109s for escort duties. Bf 110s of the 1st Destroyer Wing were occasionally employed as escorts but lacked the maneuverability needed for the role. The Germans relied on the 3rd Fighter Wing's detachment of Bf 109s at Pitomnik to link up with incoming transports, although the poor organization of radio communications and foggy weather conditions often prevented successful rendezvous. The Pitomnik detachment was constantly diverted from escort operations to defend their base against incessant VVS attacks and to support the defenses of the Sixth Army perimeter. By the middle of December VVS fighters had proven such a threat to the airlift that the VIII Air Corps decided to abandon clear weather flights and operate only when there was adequate cloud cover or at night. On days of poor visibility and low cloud ceilings crews with instrument-flying experience could fly in groups of five, while the rest flew alone or at most in groups of two to three aircraft. Aircraft always flew alone during night transport operations.

A VVS fighter pilot
prepares for a patrol.
During December, Soviet
fighters were able to
challenge and ultimately
halt German clear
weather air supply flights.
VVS aircrew benefited
from better tactics, radio-
equipped fighters, and
ground control directions
provided by the radio
monitoring and intercept
network Novikov
established behind the
front lines. (Courtesy of
the Central Museum of the
Armed Forces, Moscow,
via Stavka)

A VVS fighter pilot prepares for a patrol. During December, Soviet fighters were able to challenge and ultimately halt German clear weather air supply flights. VVS aircrew benefited from better tactics, radio-equipped fighters, and ground control directions provided by the radio monitoring and intercept network Novikov established behind the front lines. (Courtesy of the Central Museum of the Armed Forces, Moscow, via Stavka)

VIII Air Corps in command: December 1–11

Due to the threat posed by Soviet ground attacks, the VIII Corps headquarters evacuated Oblivskaya Airfield the same day and set up at Tatsinskaya. To further spur delivery operations, Richthofen reinforced his two specialized He 111 transport units, Bomber Group 5 and the newly arrived Group 20, with the 4th Air Fleet's other He 111 bomber units. Fifty percent of the He 111s were operational and available to fly. By December 3, the transport force consisted of 244 Ju 52s, 94 He 111s, and 31 Ju 86s, augmented by small numbers of Rumanian and Italian transports. Luftwaffe ground staff worked intensely to keep the number of transports operational despite the loss of support equipment to the Soviet November offensive and the limited facilities at the overcrowded airfields, and an average of 136 transports were operational daily during the first 11 days of December.

The first weeks of December should have been favorable for the airlift. The command structure was established, the transport force assembled, and the Luftwaffe did not yet have to dedicate resources to support Manstein's *Winter Storm* relief attack, which was delayed until December 12. Despite these advantages, the airlift struggled to generate sorties and get supplies through to the pocket. The minimum requirements were only met on the 7th, the airlift's overall best day, when 135 transports successfully landed at Pitomnik delivering 326.2 tons of supplies. On the 8th and 11th, deliveries exceeded 200 tons, and on three other days 100. As feared, the weather complicated flight operations, and on December 3 snowfall, fog, and temperatures around 0 degrees limited flights to two Ju 52 crews who tried to penetrate the fog but were shot down before reaching Pitomnik. Poor weather completely shut down transport flights on December 9.

The Soviet air blockade

The VVS rapidly identified the airlift as a key target. 16th VA commander General-Mayor Rudenko began ordering his fighters to intercept airlift flights as early as November 28 and launched repeated bombing raids against German airfields within the pocket. On November 30, VVS commander Novikov ordered Rudenko to dedicate one fighter and one ground attack regiment to operations against the transports. Four days later Novikov directed a more comprehensive approach, creating an air blockade structure to integrate the efforts of the 8th, 16th, and 17th Air Armies and the fighters of the 102nd Air Defense Division. He established four air blockade zones. The outermost encompassed the Luftwaffe's staging airfields, to be attacked by bombers and ground attack aircraft primarily drawn from the 17th VA and the bombers of Long-Range Aviation. The second zone was divided into five sectors, each allocated to specific units. The 8th VA patrolled the three southern sectors, the 16th the two to the north. The third zone was a belt 5–10 miles wide reserved for Soviet anti-aircraft guns. A total of 235 medium and light and 241 machine guns controlled by the Stalingrad Air Defense (PVO) Corps and ground force units were posted in the area. The final zone encompassed the Stalingrad pocket itself, where the 8th and 16th Air Armies and bombers of Long-Range Aviation conducted frequent raids against Pitomnik. German pilots reported that they were most vulnerable to Soviet fighters when caught approaching or taking off from Pitomnik.

The second-zone sectors were assigned to dedicated interceptor units, allowing the pilots and crews to become familiar with their areas of operation. "Free hunter" fighters flown by more experienced VVS pilots patrolled these areas searching for transports to engage. Novikov also used the improved VVS command and control network to increase the effectiveness of the blockade. Most Soviet aircraft were now equipped with radio sets with both transmitters and receivers, and the VVS established a control system during the autumn fighting that used radio communications and radar to monitor operations and guide Soviet fighters to their targets. Novikov set up a headquarters at Kotluban Airfield to control air operations for the blockade and vector in 8th and 16th Air Army fighters against the transports.

The Soviets employed both 37mm and 85mm guns to engage enemy aircraft at low and medium altitude in the anti-aircraft gun zone. Although the German transports tried to vary their routes to avoid the heaviest fire, the location of the launching airfields and the homing beacons at Pitomnik helped the Soviets mass their AAA batteries along the most likely routes. German Ju 52s trying to fly low to use cloud cover to avoid enemy fighters

A Soviet 37mm anti-aircraft gun in action. Novikov's air blockade included a 5–10-mile-wide zone around the pocket for 85mm and 37mm anti-aircraft guns, augmented by numbers of AAA machine guns. The Luftwaffe lacked the aircraft to strike Soviet AAA positions and resorted to varying the routes of its transports to try to evade anti-aircraft fire, lengthening the time the transports had to spend in the air. (Courtesy of the Central Museum of the Armed Forces, Moscow, via Stavka)

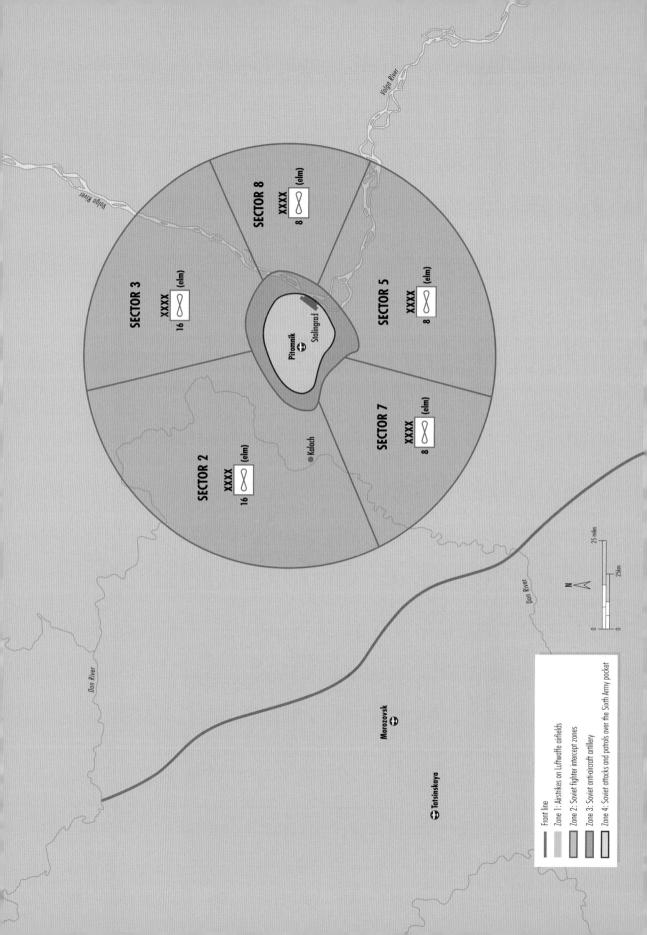

Volga River

Volga River

Don River

Don River

SECTOR 3
XXXX
16 (elm)

SECTOR 8
XXXX
8 (elm)

SECTOR 5
XXXX
8 (elm)

SECTOR 2
XXXX
16 (elm)

SECTOR 7
XXXX
8 (elm)

Pitomnik
Stalingrad

Kalach

Morozovsk

Tatsinskaya

Don River

N

0   25km
0   25 miles

Front line
Zone 1: Airstrikes on Luftwaffe airfields
Zone 2: Soviet fighter intercept zones
Zone 3: Soviet anti-aircraft artillery
Zone 4: Soviet attacks and patrols over the Sixth Army pocket

OPPOSITE SOVIET AIR BLOCKADE ZONES, EARLY DECEMBER, 1942

were more vulnerable to the ground fire, and Soviet batteries could engage aircraft flying in fog based on engine noise. The anti-aircraft batteries were difficult for the Luftwaffe to identify and attack due to snowstorms, clouds, and ground-level fog, and in any case the 4th Air Fleet could spare few resources for suppression attacks.

The VVS air blockade inflicted steady attrition on the Luftwaffe's transport force. Five Ju 52s, five He 111s, and an Italian BR.20M Fiat were lost on December 6 – a day when 44 transports successfully reached Pitomnik. The next day, the airlift delivered a record 326 tons with 135 transports landing, but suffered the loss of eight Ju 52s, a Rumanian Ju 52, and six He 111s. The Soviet 181st Fighter Regiment's commander and a pilot from the 131st both claimed double kills, and one Ju 52 fell to an Il-2. When caught unescorted, the slow Ju 52s proved vulnerable to Shturmoviks. Overall, roughly 50 Ju 52s were lost in the first month of the airlift. The outnumbered but veteran German pilots in their Bf 109s continued to exact a heavy toll from the VVS, however, claiming 34 Soviet aircraft downed in the Stalingrad and Don bend region on November 30 alone.

The VVS launched frequent attacks on the airfields both in and outside the pocket. Pickert conceded the "awe inspiring" effect of repeated waves of six to ten Soviet aircraft attacking Pitomnik on November 30, although he added the damage caused was often minimal. On December 3, lend-lease US-built Boston light bombers from the 221st Bomber Aviation Division began attacks on Tatsinskaya and Morozovsk. The 221st destroyed ten German aircraft in raids on Tatsinskaya on December 8 and 9, including four Ju 52s, and hit the airfield's fuel and ammunition dumps. The Bostons continued raids for the next two weeks, disrupting airfield operations but hitting few aircraft apart from three Ju 86s that were damaged at Tatsinskaya on December 21. The raids forced the Luftwaffe to augment the Flak defenses at the airfields and divert fighters to airfield defense.

The 4th Air Fleet was also faced with the need to help the Sixth Army and Army Group Don defend against Soviet ground attacks. The 5th Tank Army pressure on the XXXXVIII

A German tank being prepared for winter operations. The best chance for the Sixth Army once it was ordered to stand fast was a relief column, but Hitler diverted one of the three assigned panzer divisions to another task and was reluctant to reinforce Army Group Don with forces from Army Group A in the Caucasus. (Nik Cornish at www.Stavka.org.uk)

Ju 52s in flight. VVS pilots preferred to engage the slow and poorly armed Ju 52s rather than the more capable He 111s. (Nik Cornish at www.Stavka.org.uk)

General Aleksandr Vasilevskiy, Chief of the Soviet General Staff, here seen with Marshal Budenny, one of Stalin's cronies from the Civil War. Vasilevskiy deftly orchestrated Soviet operations at Stalingrad and was instrumental in shaping the response to the threat posed by Manstein's *Winter Storm* offensive. (Wikimedia-PD)

Panzer Corps defending the Chir River was so intense that Manstein had to pull it from its planned role in the attack to rescue the Sixth Army. On December 7, Richthofen removed his 3rd Fighter Wing Bf 109s off transport escort duties to aid Stukas aiding the Chir defenses. Six Bf 109s were lost in low-level strafing attacks on the attackers. The next day, Rokossovsky's Don Front attacked the Sixth Army's northwestern perimeter, and He 111s were shifted from transport roles to support the pocket with bombing attacks. Sixty Soviet tanks were reported destroyed, many by air attack. Richthofen recalled more Destroyer Group 1 Bf 110s in from the Caucasus to Tatsinskaya to reinforce air escort, as his Bf 109s were being pulled to so many other missions.

Fiebig flew into the pocket on the 11th to consult with Paulus and the Sixty Army staff, the first in a series of increasingly acrimonious interchanges between the services. The airlift had only met the minimum requirements on a single day, and Paulus stated that at such levels "my Army can neither fight nor exist." The troops were running short of ammunition, particularly shells for the divisional 105mm howitzer batteries, and Soviet troops walked openly in front of German lines as ammunition had to be conserved for major attacks. Deliveries of fuel did not even meet daily requirements, and the Sixth Army was unable to build the reserves needed for a breakout attack. With little food being flown in, the army was slaughtering its horses, and rations had been reduced on November 23 and December 8. Paulus told Fiebig the troops had now been issued their emergency rations that would last two days, and the Sixth Army staff estimated all food would be gone on December 16. The defending positions to the north, west, and south sides of the pocket were only lines of foxholes in the snow in the open steppe with few bunkers or shelters, and the health of the underfed troops was deteriorating. The first deaths from malnutrition were reported on the 21st.

Logistics and readiness problems, the weather, and Soviet opposition had already combined to cripple the airlift in its first weeks. The Luftwaffe had managed to fly in 1,442 tons of supplies during the first 11 days of December, an average of 131 tons a day, less than half of the Sixth Army's minimum requirement. Over 92 percent of the deliveries were fuel and ammunition, with seven percent rations and one percent miscellaneous gear. Despite the record 362.6 tons delivered on the 7th, no flights were able to get through due to weather conditions on the 3rd and 9th. Of a total force of over 400 transports assigned to the 4th Air Fleet, only an average of 136 aircraft were operational daily, and of these only an average of 82 took off and 62 successfully arrived each day.

Novikov's newly established air blockade zones were inflicting steady attrition both in the air and with its frequent attacks on German airfields. The VIII Air Corps staff estimated that for every ten transports sent to Stalingrad, only six were likely to reach Pitomnik and three or four to safely return. Of the two Ju 86 air groups hastily assembled and sent to Tatsinskaya, one recorded the loss of 18 aircraft to enemy action between December 6 and 12. Due to the VVS fighter threat, the Luftwaffe would abandon clear weather daylight flights in mid-December and try to avoid interception by flying only at night or in cloudy conditions. At this point, the airlift was clearly incapable of adequately supplying the pocket, and the only hope for the Sixth Army lay with Manstein's plan to break through with a relief force.

Winter Storm (Wintergewitter), Thunderclap (Donnerschlag), and Little Saturn (Molnyy Saturn)

While the Luftwaffe struggled to get supplies through to the Sixth Army, Manstein was trying to gather adequate forces to launch his relief operation, codenamed *Winter Storm*. The initial plan included two separate thrusts towards the pocket. The XXXXVIII Panzer Corps, located on the Chir around 40 miles from Stalingrad, would attack directly west, while the LVII Panzer Corps with the 6th, 17th, and 23rd Panzer Divisions would strike northeast from Kotelnikovo. The weak VI and VII Rumanian Corps would guard the LVII's flanks. Although it had to cover 68 miles to reach the Sixth Army, Manstein hoped that the LVII's attack would achieve surprise. Eight hundred trucks with 3,000 tons of supplies followed the panzer spearhead to provide the Sixth Army with a rapid infusion of supplies once the pocket was reached. The Sixth Army was ordered to prepare Operation *Donnerschlag* (*Thunderclap*) to break through the encircling Soviet troops and meet the relief force. Events intervened to delay and weaken the attack, however. Hitler held the 17th Panzer Division in the north, and Soviet attacks against the Chir forced the XXXXVIII Panzer onto the defensive. Despite these setbacks, Manstein felt he could no longer delay and *Winter Storm*, now reduced to a two Panzer division attack, began on December 12.

Soviet fighters attack Ju 52 transports, Stalingrad, 1942

The Luftwaffe ran into increasing difficulties trying to escort transports to the Stalingrad pocket in early December. On December 11, the Soviet 9th Guards Fighter Regiment intercepted 18 Ju 52 transports with Bf 109 escorts. The 9th was a specially organized elite unit staffed with experienced pilots, equipped with new Yak-1s with full radio sets, and trained in the new four- and two-ship *para-zveno* tactics. The 9th rendezvoused with the La-5-equipped 3rd Guards Fighter Regiment, also a capable unit.

Eight of the Ju 52s broke off and dashed for their home bases, but the pilots of the 9th were able to shoot down four Ju 52s, and the 3rd Guards six others. In the foreground, a Ju 52 tries to escape attack while a 9th Guards Yak-1 pulls up after a firing pass. To the rear, one of the Bf 109 escorts tries to evade a pursuing 3rd Guards La-5. The action took place in the Soviet air blockade's third zone, generally reserved for anti-aircraft fire, but the Soviet fighters braved the zone to engage the transports, and shells are bursting among the action.

Novikov's air blockade posed a severe challenge to the VIII Air Corps' efforts to fly transports into the Stalingrad pocket in clear weather. The Bf 109 escorts had difficulties staying with the slow Ju 52s and lacked the range to escort the transports all the way to Pitomnik. The VVS's radio monitoring system was effective at vectoring in fighters on the transports, and after heavy losses the Luftwaffe abandoned clear weather daylight transport flights in mid-December, relying instead on flights at night or when the conditions provided enough cloud or fog cover to conceal the Ju 52s and He 111s. The VVS had won the first round for air superiority only weeks into the airlift.

Il-2 Shturmoviks in formation. The 17th Air Army's Il-2s suffered heavy losses to the Luftwaffe at the beginning of Operation *Little Saturn* due to the late arrival of assigned VVS fighter units. (Photo by Sovfoto/Universal Images Group via Getty Images)

Hopes were high that Luftwaffe air support could provide the weakened *Winter Storm* attack force with additional punch. Manstein and Richthofen, the team that led the powerful air-ground assault on Sevastopol, would be working together again. Unlike at Sevastopol, however, Richthofen's 4th Air Fleet would not be able to focus its striking power as support to *Winter Storm* would need to be balanced with the airlift, Sixth Army, and the Chir defenses. Richthofen kept Fiebig in control of the supply flights to the pocket with half of the 4th Air Fleet's fighters, but the VIII Air Corps' He 111s would be shifted from transport duties to support *Winter Storm*. Fiebig did not protest, confiding to his diary that the relief was much more vital than "a few additional tons in the fortress." Stukas and some fighters were kept to support the Chir defenses, although their readiness was only around 35–40 percent, and Richthofen had to augment them with what was left of the small Rumanian air element. Pflugbeil's IV Air Corps headquarters would control the air support to the LVII Panzer Corps. The IV had two Stuka, one ground attack, and one destroyer (Bf 110) wings, adequate for attacks in support of the panzers but with insufficient fighter power to match VVS fighters and Shturmoviks should they intervene. The IV suffered the same readiness problems as other Luftwaffe units and had only approximately 200 aircraft operational on any given day to support the attack.

The LVII Panzer Corps attack began in the early hours of December 12, led by its 230 white-painted tanks. IV Air Corps Bf 110s began the day with a raid on Abganerovo, the main Soviet air base in the sector, destroying eight aircraft caught on the ground. Stuka Groups 1 and 77, and Bf 110s of Destroyer Group 1 struck Soviet defensive positions to open a path for the panzer divisions, while Ju 88s and He 111s hit Red Army lines of communication covered by Fighter Group 52's Bf 109s. The attack on the Kotelnikovo axis surprised the weakened Soviet 51st Army and rapidly overran its forward defenses. German attacking forces advanced up to 35 miles on the 12th and seized a bridge over the Aksay River in the early hours of the offensive's second day. The VVS initially kept the 8th and 16th Air Armies focused on maintaining the air blockade around the pocket, and Soviet support to the Red Army defenders was ineffectual. The Germans claimed 54 enemy aircraft destroyed, half on the ground, at the cost of half a dozen. At the same time, 69 transports took off and 56 were able to land at Potomik on the 12th, but as many as ten Ju 52s and eight He 111s were lost to the air blockade. An additional Italian Fiat BR.20M and a Ju 86 were also shot down, the latter to a 9th Guards "ace regiment" pilot who misidentified the uncommon aircraft as a Do 215.

Richthofen personally threw himself into galvanizing Luftwaffe support for the *Winter Storm* attack, flying in his Storch to several air units as well as the Army Group Don and LVII Panzer headquarters on the 13th. The day began with strong air support to the attacking panzers, but attacks by the 5th Tank and newly formed 5th Shock Armies forced Richthofen to shift some airpower back to the Chir front later in the day. Poor weather on the 14th reduced air support to the LVII Panzer Corps assault, and the 51st Army was able to hold the Germans halfway between the Aksay and Myshkova Rivers. Five days of intense fighting ensued as the 6th and 23rd Panzer Divisions battled Soviet units reinforcing the 51st Army and trying to force the Germans back to the Aksay.

Little Saturn

Stalin and his high command had been planning an ambitious follow-on offensive since early December aimed at seizing Rostov and trapping Army Group A in the Caucasus. The realization that the pocket contained over 250,000 troops rather than the first Soviet estimates of 95,000 and the progress of the *Winter Storm* relief attack led to the hasty revision of what had been codenamed Operation *Saturn*. Colonel-General Aleksandr M. Vasilevsky, Chief of the General Staff, convinced a reluctant Stalin that the 2nd Guards Army must be shifted from its planned role in the offensive and moved south to halt *Winter Storm*. As a result, Saturn was recast as *Molnyy* (*Little*) *Saturn*, and the objective shifted from a deep strike on Rostov to the envelopment of the Army Group Don forces defending the Chir River. The initial target of the new plan was the Italian 8th Army's defenses on the Don, and once they were penetrated, two tank corps were to strike deep and raid the airfields at Tatsinskaya and Morozovsk. Like the other Axis satellite forces, the Italians had weak anti-tank capabilities, and their AMIR aviation force now consisted of 81 aircraft that were crippled by fuel and spare parts shortages. The VVS's 17th Air Army had 632 aircraft to support the attack

Stukas awaiting loading for a strike mission. Stukas and other 4th Air Fleet aircraft provided close support to the LVII Panzer Corps, allowing it to reach a point 30 miles from the pocket on December 19. (Nik Cornish at www.Stavka.org.uk)

Operation *Winter Storm* is unleashed, December 12, 1942

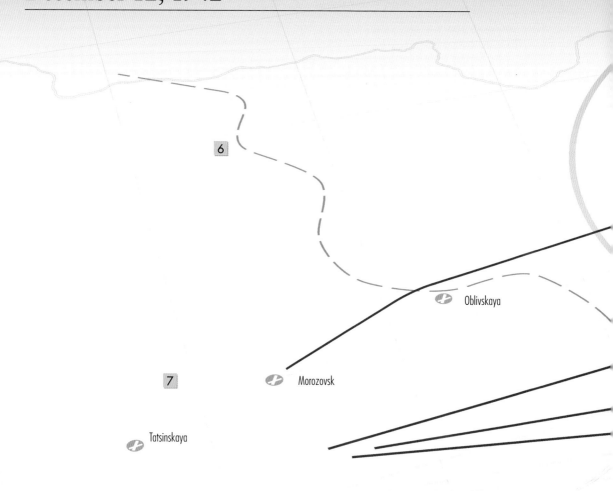

EVENTS

1. Manstein launches Operation *Winter Storm*. The LVII Panzer Corps strikes from Kotelnikovo with two Panzer Divisions, aiming to establish a land corridor to the Stalingrad pocket 68 miles to the north. Richthofen assigns his IV Air Corps under Pflugbeil to support *Winter Storm* with two Stuka groups (1st and 77th), a ground attack group (1st) and Luftwaffe Bf 110s of 1st Destroyer Group (ZG 1).

2. Bf 110s begin the attack by launching a strike on the main Soviet airfield in the area at Abganerovo, destroying eight planes on the ground, including four Il-2s of the 811th Shturmovik Ground Attack Regiment.

3. The Stukas and ground attack aircraft strike the weak Soviet 51st Army's defenses and play a key role in helping the LVII Panzer Corps break through. Some of the armored units cover over 30 miles on the first day and secure crossings over the Aksay River in the early hours of the second day of the offensive.

4. Richthofen assigns additional aircraft from the VIII Air Corps to support *Winter Storm*. Bf 109s, Ju 88s, He 111s, and some Rumanian dive-bombers strike lines of communication targets in the Stalingrad Front rear areas.

5. The Soviets are slow to react to the attack both on the ground and in the air, and the 8th and 17th Air Armies remain focused on December 12 air blockade operations against the Stalingrad airlift. The Luftwaffe's shift of resources to *Winter Storm* reduces its efforts to resupply Stalingrad; only 55 aircraft land in the pocket on December 12. The Germans lose ten Ju 52s, eight He 111s, and one Ju 86 on December 12, along with an Italian Fiat BR.20M.

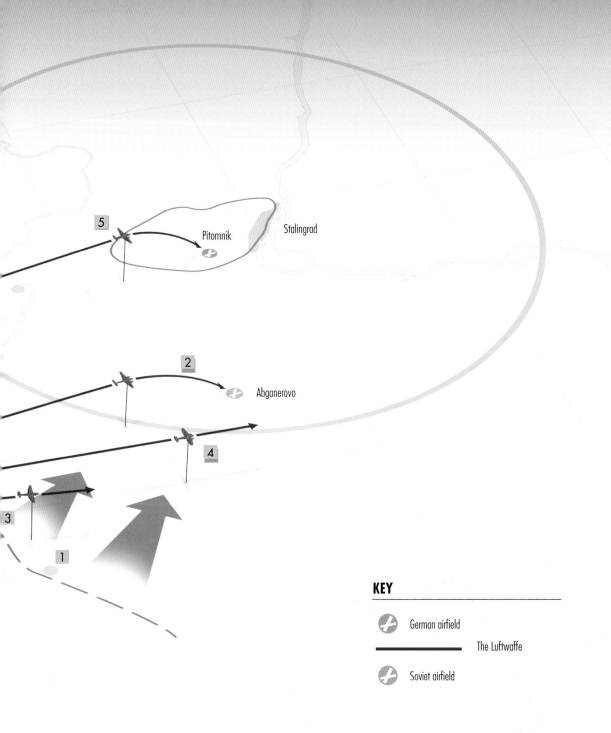

KEY

⊕ German airfield

———————— The Luftwaffe

⊕ Soviet airfield

EVENTS

6. The German *Winter Storm* attack will lead the Soviets to transform their planned Operation *Saturn* offensive, a major attack aimed at Rostov, into the smaller *Little Saturn* attack aimed at breaking through the lines of the Eighth Italian Army just to the north of the map area shown on the Don River. The attack will be launched on December 16.

7. By December 20–25, the advancing Soviet *Little Saturn* offensive will force the Luftwaffe to evacuate Morozovsk and the 24th Tank Corps will raid Tatsinskaya. By early January, the Luftwaffe will be forced to abandon Tatsinskaya and Morozovsk, crippling its ability to resupply the Sixth Army in Stalingrad.

The Soviet tank raid on Tatsinskaya destroyed numbers of aircraft on the field and disrupted the airlift. No transports reached the pocket on the day of the raid, and only seven on the next. (Nik Cornish at www.Stavka.org.uk)

The Soviet tank raid on Tatsinskaya destroyed numbers of aircraft on the field and disrupted the airlift. No transports reached the pocket on the day of the raid, and only seven on the next. (Nik Cornish at www.Stavka.org.uk)

although not all of its assigned fighters had arrived. Stalin nevertheless insisted that the assault begin as scheduled on the 16th.

Poor weather limited the 17th VA to 200 sorties when the assault began against the Italian lines. The Luftwaffe rapidly engaged with the forces at hand to support the Italians, and the Soviets suffered heavy Il-2 Shturmovik losses to the Bf 109s of Fighter Group 52. Six Henschel Hs-129 attack aircraft of *Schlacht* (Attack) Group I claimed ten Soviet tanks destroyed with their MK 101 anti-tank cannon on the 16th and 17th. The Luftwaffe claimed a total of 14 tanks and 28 Soviet aircraft destroyed during the first two days of the Soviet offensive. Both sides rushed to augment their air assets over the *Little Saturn* battlefront. 4th Air Fleet pulled forces from *Winter Storm*, dispatching a squadron of Bf 110s from its 1st Destroyer Wing and Stukas from Stuka Wing 77. A Luftwaffe bomber group was even dispatched from Army Group Center to help the Italians. The VVS moved to shore up its fighter cover, dispatching an additional fighter division to help cover its Il-2s. Both sides recorded successes in the air during the *Little Saturn* fighting. The 9th Guards "regiment of aces" claimed two Bf 109s, two 110s, one He 111, and an Fw 189 reconnaissance aircraft on December 17, with all but one of the Bf 109 claims substantiated in German reports. Overall, however, German experience in the air gave them the advantage over the less well-trained Soviets, and Fighter Group 53 claimed 27 VVS aircraft.

The Italian forces held the line against the *Little Saturn* offensive for two days, but the weight of the Soviet attack eventually began to tell. The 17th VA, now strengthened by additional fighters, provided strong support in the air and the 3rd Guards Army joined the attack on the ground. Soon, three of the Italian divisions were encircled, and by the fourth day of the offensive a 100-mile gap had been torn in the front. Ultimately, 50,000 Italians would enter Soviet prisoner-of-war camps. The Soviet tank corps moved through the penetration and began to drive south to attack Tatsinskaya and Morozovsk.

The climax

Manstein reinvigorated the *Winter Storm* attack, gambling that the LVII Panzer Corps could reach Stalingrad before the *Little Saturn* attack broke through. On the 19th the 17th Panzer Division at last arrived to reinforce the assault, and groups of 20–30 aircraft supported each divisional attack column. Other Luftwaffe aircraft struck and delayed the 2nd Guards Army as it moved south to reinforce the 51st. The panzers at last broke through and reached the Myskova River, only 30 miles from Stalingrad. In response, the 8th and 16th VAs were shifted from air blockade duties to assist the desperate 51st Army. Aircraft of the 16th flew 523 combat sorties on December 19, at the cost of 12 aircraft, and its fighters were able to clear the skies for repeated Il-2 Shturmovik strikes on the panzers.

In the face of renewed VVS air strikes and the arrival of the 2nd Guards Army, the LVII Panzer Corps' assault ground to a halt on the Myskova. Manstein sought permission for the Sixth Army to launch Operation *Thunderclap* to meet the relief column, but during a series of conferences over the next several days between Paulus, Manstein, and Hitler, the Führer insisted the Sixth Army retain all its positions in Stalingrad. For their part, Paulus and his staff were concerned about their army's

Russian Pe-2s on an attack run. Pe-2s using dive-bombing techniques were able to hit their targets with increased accuracy and played an important role in Soviet attacks on Kotelnikovo in late 1942. (Courtesy of the Central Museum of the Armed Forces, Moscow, via Stavka)

mobility. To build up its fuel reserves Paulus had sought the delivery of 200 cubic meters of fuel a day since the start of the airlift. Although fuel supplies were the priority, the Luftwaffe was only able to fly in an average of 37 cubic meters, not enough to cover even daily requirements. The *Winter Storm* force was 30 miles away, close enough so that the lead troops could see artillery fire around the pocket reflected in the night sky, but Paulus reported that his troops had only enough fuel for 20 miles. By December 22, Manstein was forced to pull forces from the stalled relief attempt and the Chir River defenses to protect Tatsinskaya and Morozovsk, leaving the LVII Panzer Corps with only 19 operational tanks. Hitler reaffirmed his "stand fast" orders for the Sixth Army and promised yet more armored divisions to reinvigorate the relief attempt. These reinforcements would not arrive for weeks, however, and the Soviet assault against the Italians had broken through. It was clear that *Winter Storm* had failed.

German Hs 129 *Schlacht* aircraft attack Soviet tanks, December 16, 1942

Throughout the 71 days of the airlift, the Luftwaffe faced intense demands on its limited resources to support its hard-pressed ground forces as it tried to fly supplies to the Stalingrad pocket. While the 4th Air Fleet was devoting all available support to Manstein's *Winter Storm* offensive to break through to Paulus, the Soviets launched Operation *Little Saturn* on December 16 against the Italian Eighth Army on the Don River. Like all of the German allied forces during the campaign, the Italians were spread thin, lacked reserves, and did not have adequate anti-tank weaponry to cope with Soviet armor. The Luftwaffe diverted all available aircraft to support the Italians.

Although it has the reputation of a consummate ground support air force, the Luftwaffe had relatively small numbers of wings in its order of battle specifically designated "Schlacht" (attack), exclusively organized for close air support. In 1942, the wings were equipped with small numbers of Bf 109E/Bs outfitted for ground attack, and the specialized Hs 123 biplane and Hs 129 ground attack aircraft. The Hs 129 had an armored "bathtub" much like the Il-2 Shturmovik, but the initial production model was considered underpowered. After the fall of France, the Hs 129B version was outfitted with more powerful French Gnome-Rhône 14M engines.

In the battle scene two Hs 129s of the 4th Air Group/1st Attack Wing attack Soviet armored columns using their MK 101 centerline 30mm cannon. The Luftwaffe claimed a total of 14 tanks and 28 aircraft destroyed on the first two days of the Soviet offensive. German air support helped the Italians hold out for several days, but the weight of Soviet ground and air attacks eventually smashed the 8th Army's defenses, and the Red Army was able to exploit the breakthrough to send two tank corps to raid the primary Luftwaffe airlift fields at Tatsinskaya and Morozovsk.

The airlift, December 12–23

The VIII Air Corps strove hard to keep up supply flights to Pitomnik despite the diversion of forces to support the Chir, the LVII Panzer Corps, and the Italian Eighth Army. The Soviet air armies initially remained focused on maintaining the air blockade, and fighters of the 230th Division claimed ten aircraft destroyed in a December 13 raid on Pitomnik. A total of 73 transports got through on the 13th, 85 on the 14th, and 50 on the 15th, delivering a total of 360.5 tons. A total of 172 planes arrived during the next three days, delivering a total of just over 300 tons of supplies, amounts so low that on the 18th the Sixth Army chief of staff, General Schmidt, radioed Fiebig demanding that the Luftwaffe step up its deliveries. The diversion of the 8th and 16th Air Armies' aircraft to meet the threat posed by *Winter Storm* on December 19 reduced opposition to airlift flights for the next four days, and over 100 transports landed each day, delivering almost 850 tons – an average of 212 tons a day. The Sixth Army's minimum requirements had, for the first time, almost been reached for a period of consecutive days. With fewer Soviet fighters flying in the blockade zones, losses were lighter – on December 20, 100 He 111s and 80 Ju 52s and Ju 86s landed at Pitomnik, delivering 220 tons of supplies, suffering only two Ju 86s, two He 111s, and a Ju 52 damaged, and 144 transports delivered over 300 tons the next day.

Hitler not only promised additional reinforcements to restart a ground relief attempt, but he also ordered 4,000 tons of fuel and 1,800 tons of rations be immediately flown into the pocket – an impossible task given the challenges Fiebig's transports were already facing. At the airlift's current rate, such resupply would take 40 days, assuming no consumption of the supplies flown in. Fiebig characterized the order as "simply impossible to accomplish." When one of Manstein's staff flew into the pocket, Paulus' chief of staff asserted that "The Sixth Army will be in position in Easter. You only have to supply it better." Even the Luftwaffe's ability to deliver limited amounts of supplies to the pocket would now be threatened, however, as the *Little Saturn* exploitation force began to move to raid Tatsinskaya and Morozovsk.

The raid on Tatsinskaya, December 24

With the collapse of the Italian Eighth Army, the Soviet 24th and 25th Tank Corps began moving south to raid the airfields and Fiebig requested permission to evacuate if necessary. Both airfields were packed with transports as well as vital ground support equipment, especially fuel trucks and the *Warmewagen* heaters needed to start the engines during the severe winter weather. Göring had played almost no role in leading the airlift to date, but now intervened to order that the airfields be held until under direct tank fire, claiming that an evacuation would hurt morale in the pocket. Richthofen ordered 30 Ju 52s to Salsk on the 23rd to ease the crowding at Tatsinskaya, but as four of the first nine crashed due to poor weather Fiebig halted the departure of the remainder.

The approach march of the Soviet tank corps was dogged by difficult terrain and vehicle breakdowns. The 24th Tank Corps was reduced on the march from 200 to 80 tanks but took Tatsinskaya under fire during the early morning hours of December 24. Fiebig only had two 88mm and four 20mm anti-aircraft guns available for local defense as most of the airfield's Flak had already been sent to reinforce other units, and the first Soviet rounds destroyed the airfield's signals building. After some hesitation, Fiebig launched a chaotic evacuation by both ground

Burning Ju-88s at an airfield in the Soviet Union. The Soviets inflicted heavy losses on Luftwaffe aircraft at their bases, both by frequent air raids and the December 24 tank raid on Tatsinskaya, which destroyed about 50 of the transports at the airfield. (Nik Cornish at www.Stavka.org.uk)

and air elements in the teeth of the Soviet tank fire. Falling snow and limited visibility – 300 meters and a ceiling of 30 meters – both complicated the takeoffs and may have helped limit the effectiveness of the incoming Soviet fire. Fiebig and members of his senior staff departed in the last Ju 52 to take off, the pilot dodging the numerous burning wrecks littering the runway. In all 108 Ju 52s and 16 Ju 86s were able to get away, leaving roughly 50 aircraft destroyed on the field. Losses included 22 Ju 52s, 24 Ju 86s, and four Ju 88s. All the fuel trucks and warming equipment was lost at the field along with tons of supplies stockpiled for delivery to the Sixth Army and 300 tons of aviation fuel.

The parallel thrust by the 25th Tank Corps against Morozovsk met with less success. Oberst Ernst Kühl flew his He 111s off to Novocherkassk on the 23rd without waiting for permission while he remained at the base with a small staff. Kühl exploited the good flying weather over Christmas to call in his bombers and pummel the enemy tanks stalled on the open steppe about 10 miles away with the He 111 horizonal bombers delivering strikes from low altitudes. Soviet doctrine and command and control for deep penetration operations by mechanized units was still immature, and both the 24th and 25th Tank Corps suffered from poor communications and could not obtain air cover. With the 25th Tank Corps repulsed, Kühl called his bombers back to Morozovsk on the day after Christmas. Although the Soviet tank attacks had been planned as hit-and-run raids, Stalin decided that possession of Tatsinskaya had propaganda value and ordered the 24th Tank Corps to remain and hold the airfield. Manstein shifted the 11th Panzer Division from the Chir to retake the base, and after a four-day encirclement the remnants of the 24th had to break out and retreat north.

OPPOSITE GERMAN RETREAT TO ROSTOV

Although the cost to the raiding tank corps had been high, the raid had a profound impact on the airlift. Escaping Ju 52s had scattered to a variety of bases, and the command and control and airfield support infrastructure was disrupted. No transports flew to the pocket on the 24th, and only seven, delivering nine tons of supplies, on Christmas day. It would take several days for the Luftwaffe to reorganize and restart operations. Taking off from their new base at Salsk, 37 Ju 52s were able to deliver 78 tons of supplies on December 26, but five were shot down and the Soviets claim to have destroyed eight more on the ground. As it reorganized, the Luftwaffe also faced the additional mission of airdropping supplies to the 298th Infantry Division and several Italian divisions now encircled by the *Little Saturn* offensive.

Although recaptured by the 11th Panzer, Tatsinskaya would change hands several times during the next week and was never used again as an airlift base. Richthofen's staff regrouped the Ju 52s at Salsk. With *Winter Storm* facing defeat, the transport pilots scrambled to restart sorties, and 96 reached the pocket on December 29, delivering 124 tons of supplies. The cost was high, with ten transports damaged or lost, including an SM.81 carrying wounded and General Enrico Pezzi, the commander of the Italian Expeditionary Air Force, as he was returning from the pocket. For the next several days, the Luftwaffe managed close to 100 sorties a day and flew out 4,120 personnel, mostly wounded. Morozovsk was used by the He 111s until January 1 when abandoned due to Soviet advances.

Prospects were grim for the Sixth Army as the year ended, and the entire position of German forces in the southern USSR was precarious. Hitler remained determined to hold Stalingrad, the one clear accomplishment of the costly summer campaign, and continued to cling to plans to restart an attack to relieve the pocket. On December 27, he informed Manstein that he was dispatching the SS Wiking and 7th Panzer Divisions and a battalion of new Tiger tanks to allow a renewed push, although it would be weeks before they could arrive. Events at the front soon outpaced any hope that Hitler's plans for the new divisions would make a difference for the Sixth Army. The 2nd Guards Army was now fully able to bring its

As the VIII Air Corps was driven back from Tatsinskaya and Morozovsk to airfields further from Stalingrad in late December, the Luftwaffe high command sent small numbers of longer-ranged aircraft to reinforce the effort. A composite air group was stationed at Stalino with 28 Fw 200 Condor maritime reconnaissance aircraft and two Ju 290 long-range transports. The Condors had long range and could carry five tons but were difficult to maintain and ultimately proved unsuccessful. (Nik Cornish at www.Stavka.org.uk)

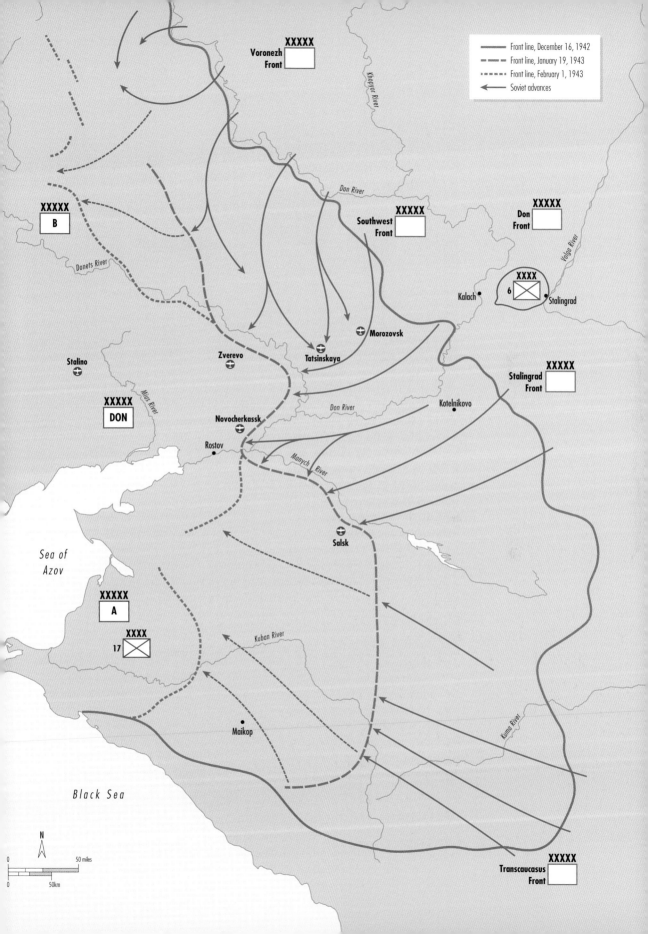

Voronezh Front XXXXX

Khopyor River

Don River

Southwest Front XXXXX

Don Front XXXXX

XXXXX
B

Volga River

Kalach •

XXXX
6 ⊠ • Stalingrad

Donets River

Stalino ⊕

Zverevo ⊕

Morozovsk ⊕

Tatsinskaya ⊕

Stalingrad Front XXXXX

XXXXX
DON

Mius River

Don River

Kotelnikovo •

Novocherkassk ⊕

Rostov •

Manych River

Salsk ⊕

Sea of Azov

XXXXX
A

XXXX
17 ⊠

Kuban River

Maikop •

Kuma River

Black Sea

Transcaucasus Front XXXXX

Legend:
— Front line, December 16, 1942
– – Front line, January 19, 1943
···· Front line, February 1, 1943
← Soviet advances

N

0 ———— 50 miles
0 ———— 50km

power to bear against the *Winter Storm* forces, and Soviet forces launched attacks against the weak Rumanian VI and VII Corps guarding the LVII Corps' flanks. The hard-won position on the Myskova River was lost, and Axis forces were driven back toward Kotelnikovo. A December 26 dive-bombing attack by Pe-2s from the 284th Bomber Aviation Regiment led by Major Dmitriy Valentik destroyed a train loaded with critically needed supplies and fuel at Kotelnikovo, weakening the defenders. Richthofen threw repeated Stuka sorties against the attacking Soviet armor, but by the end of the year the German defenders had to withdraw to positions south of the town.

Manstein was faced with crises from every direction. The LVII Panzer Corps was withdrawing to avoid encirclement, and the loss of Kotelnikovo opened a southern route for Soviet forces to advance on Salsk and Rostov; the Chir River was under constant Soviet pressure; and the Luftwaffe had been driven from Tatsinskaya and Morozovsk. The *Little Saturn* offensive had brought the Soviets closer to Rostov than the bulk of Manstein's forces, and the focus shifted from relieving Paulus to saving the entire German force in the south from destruction. The reality of the situation began to slowly penetrate even Hitler's headquarters, and on December 28 Chief of Staff Zeitzler obtained approval from a reluctant Führer to begin to withdraw Army Group A from its exposed positions in the Caucasus.

As Army Groups A and Don fought for survival, the Sixth Army could only look to the Luftwaffe for support. An average of 73 transports had arrived daily during December 12–31, delivering an average of 138 tons. By late December, with the Sixth Army's rations completely gone and little prospect of a breakout operation, resupply shifted from fuel and ammunition to food to try to keep the now-starving army fighting. With more losses to its already-overstretched logistical and ground maintenance assets, and pushed to airfields farther from the pocket, there was little prospect for Richthofen's forces to meet even the 300 tonnage minimum daily requirement.

A new year, fading hope: January 1–15, 1943

Paulus' Sixth Army had been on short rations for weeks, and with all the horses slaughtered and rations consumed deaths from malnutrition and desertions to the enemy were rising. The troops were down to 50 grams of bread a day as the new year began. Rations became top priority for resupply, but some fuel and ammunition were needed to transport and distribute the supplies, move local reserves, and sustain the defense. Just as the Sixth Army's reliance on the airlift increased, the Luftwaffe found itself more poorly positioned to support it. The Ju 52s were now operating from Salsk and the He 111s from Novocherkassk. Flying from Salsk reduced the Ju 52s' cargo-carrying capacity and increased the flight time and vulnerability to interception. The airfield was poorly set up for daily operations, and snowstorms and heavy frosts impacted readiness. Novocherkassk was 80 miles further west from Morozovsk, and the bomber-transports now had a 274-mile flight to Pitomnik. Transports were even more unlikely to fly multiple sorties a day, even if the ground crews, having suffered additional losses in personnel and equipment from the recent evacuations, could support such a turn-around rate.

Airfield	Transports supported	Dates of primary use for airlift	Distance to Stalingrad (miles)
Tatsinskaya	Ju 52, Ju 86	Nov 24–Dec 24, 1942	170
Morozovsk	He 111	Nov 24, 1942–Jan 2, 1943	140
Salsk	Ju 52	Dec 24, 1942–Jan 16, 1943	230
Novocherkassk	He 111	Jan 2–Jan 19, 1943	250
Zverevo	Ju 52	Jan 16–Feb 2, 1943	250
Stalino*	Fw 200, Ju 290, He 177	Jan 9–Feb 2, 1943	375
*Modern Donetsk; airfield remained in German hands until September 1943.			

As the bases to the west faced challenges, the Luftwaffe's ability to cover incoming transport flights from fighters at Pitomnik was steadily ground down. The detachment of the 3rd Fighter Wing at the base had been constantly engaged, striving to help cover incoming transports but daily pulled to defend troops on the perimeter and Pitomnik itself from the constant VVS strikes. The unit ultimately claimed to have downed a total of 130 Soviet aircraft, but by the end of December incessant raids and steady attrition by the 16th VA had virtually neutralized the detachment. Lt. Georg Schentke, a 90-victory ace flying from Pitomnik, was shot down and captured on December 25, a major blow to the morale of the few remaining pilots. Outside of the pocket, the 4th Air Fleet's Bf 109s had been forced to

A crashed Bf 109 fighter on a snowy airfield. The detachment of Bf 109s stationed at Pitomnik had been reduced to a handful of fighters by mid-January. On the 16th, the five remaining Bf 109s took off from Pitomnik as Soviet forces closed in and tried to land at Gumrak. Despite Sixth Army claims, the field was unready to handle air operations, and four of the Bf 109s were damaged when they hit hidden shell holes on the runway. (Nik Cornish at www.Stavka.org.uk)

Italian personnel shoveling an airfield in Russia with bombers in the background. The airfield at Zverevo used by the Ju 52s from January 16 was particularly primitive, and aircraft were packed on the narrow plowed areas around the runway. (Nik Cornish at www.Stavka.org.uk)

evacuate to airfields near Novocherkassk, allowing them to support Manstein's defenses but too far to the rear to allow any escort operations to the pocket.

The VIII Air Corps staff realized that Soviet advances would soon threaten the new Ju 52 base at Salsk and began to scout for a suitable site to construct a new field should another evacuation become necessary. They settled on a cornfield near Zverevo, about 65km north of Novocherkassk and just at the edge of the Ju 52's range to Stalingrad. While distant, it was at least for the time secure from the Red Army, and work on the new field began immediately. The hastily constructed base was the most primitive of the airfields used to support the airlift. The runway was packed snow, there were no hangars, and all aircraft maintenance had to be performed in the open. Fiebig would be forced to relocate his Ju 52s from Salsk to the improvised airfield at Zverevo on January 16. Almost no snowplows had survived the repeated airfield evacuations, and the runway was cleared and planes repeatedly dug out of snowdrifts by personnel working with shovels. The remaining engine-warming equipment was completely inadequate to start the aircraft. Despite below-zero temperatures there were only a few huts and tents, and windows in the few buildings and an old bus used for shelter were shattered by Soviet air raids, leaving them open to the cold wind. Zverevo lacked adequate anti-aircraft defenses, with only a German 37mm and a Rumanian 75mm battery, and was vulnerable to VVS raids.

In addition to problems with new bases, weather and VVS opposition continued to plague the transports. Fiebig noted in his diary that the weather conditions were so poor that most pilots would refuse to fly under normal circumstances. Roughly 30 percent of the aircraft launched had to turn back due to the weather. Sixty-two Ju 52s were reported damaged or destroyed between December 28 and January 4, with weather responsible for about half of the losses, VVS fighter and anti-aircraft fire the rest. Twenty-five He 111s and four Ju 86s were also listed as lost or severely damaged during the same period. Despite all the challenges, the Luftwaffe determined to strengthen the airlift, and additional Ju 52s and He 111s arrived at the new airfields in late December. By January 17, an airlift high of 690 transports were dedicated to the effort, although the reinforcements had limited impact due to the endemic maintenance and logistical problems, and of these only 61 were operational and ready to fly.

The surviving Ju 86s, never very effective, were withdrawn, but a variety of other aircraft joined the lift force. Much was hoped from the Fw 200 Condor, which had long range and a high carrying capacity of five tons. When used as a maritime reconnaissance asset, the Condor posed a major threat to Allied convoy operations in Atlantic and Arctic waters. Twenty-five Fw 200s were dispatched from Bomber Group 40 on the Atlantic coast, organized along with two Ju 290 airliner-transports into an amalgamated unit designated *Kampfgruppe* 200 and stationed at Stalino. During the first flight by seven Condors on January 9, they delivered 4½ tons of fuel, 9 of ammunition, and 22.5 tons of rations, and were able to return with 156 wounded. The next day saw heavy losses to the Condors, with two shot down by Soviet fighters and three crashed at Pitomnik. They continued to operate with the airlift until February 2, but during these 25 days only three of the 20–25 Condors were operational at any given time. Two Ju 290 long-range four-engine transports capable of carrying 10 tons in and 80 wounded out were dispatched and made a successful round trip on January 10. One Ju 290 crashed on takeoff from Pitomnik on the 13th, and the second Ju 290 was engaged by LaGG-3s over the pocket and was so damaged it had to be returned to Germany for repairs. Twenty-eight He 177 long-range bombers led by Major Kurt Schede joined on January 16 and operated from Stalino and Zaporozhe. The bombers were still in development and could fly long ranges but were difficult to keep operational, consumed great amounts of fuel, and suffered from in-flight engine fires. Only seven of the bombers could take off on the 16th, and Schede himself was shot down flying one of them to the pocket. Overall, the He 177s managed only 19 successful air supply missions and lost five of their number to enemy action or mechanical failure.

Despite these challenges, the augmented VIII Air Corps transport force pushed itself to fly as many supplies as possible to Pitomnik, with deliveries now almost completely composed of rations. During January 1–15 an average of 72 transports delivered 150 tons every 24 hours. Rations, followed by fuel, comprised the loads, although overall the Luftwaffe was still only delivering half of the 300-ton requirement and far short of the staff estimate of 252 tons of rations needed to feed the army every day.

In addition to the arrival of additional transports, the collapse of Operation *Winter Storm* and the success of the *Little Saturn* offensive had led Hitler to dispatch major reinforcements at last to his ground and air forces in the south. The powerful II SS Panzer Corps was dispatched from the west, although it would not arrive in time to help Stalingrad. The 4th Air Fleet, down to only 200 or so operational combat aircraft in the last weeks of 1942, received more badly needed fighters, bombers, and Stukas in early January. Six additional bomber, two Stuka, and two fighter groups arrived, and the 4th now controlled 1,150 of the 1,715 combat aircraft on the Eastern Front. The 4th Air Fleet played a key role in supporting

Generalfeldmarschall Milch with Richthofen in 1940. Hitler dispatched Milch to galvanize the Luftwaffe's airlift efforts, but he arrived at Richthofen's headquarters on January 16, too late to have much impact on the provision of supplies to the Sixth Army. (Wikimedia-PD)

OPPOSITE OPERATION *KOLTSO* AND THE DESTRUCTION OF THE SIXTH ARMY

Manstein's patched together defenses struggling to hold the front for a few vital weeks as Army Groups Don and A pulled back from their exposed positions. Richthofen's strength, however, immediately began to weaken in the intense January fighting.

The end: January 16–February 2, 1943

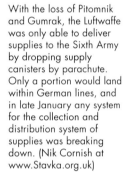

With the loss of Pitomnik and Gumrak, the Luftwaffe was only able to deliver supplies to the Sixth Army by dropping supply canisters by parachute. Only a portion would land within German lines, and in late January any system for the collection and distribution system of supplies was breaking down. (Nik Cornish at www.Stavka.org.uk)

In early January the Stavka assigned all the forces encircling the pocket to Rokossovsky's Don Front and ordered the final destruction of the Sixth Army. The 16th Air Army now controlled all air blockade operations and was assigned to support Rokossovsky's attack, while the 17th and 8th VAs supported the Soviet fronts attacking toward Rostov. Paulus had received and on Hitler's order rejected a surrender demand on January 8. Hitler insisted his troops defend to the bitter end throughout the war whatever the circumstances, but his demand that the Sixth Army fight on in January was also justified by military necessity. As long as the pocket held out it tied down Soviet forces that might otherwise be able to concentrate on the destruction of the entire German southern front. On the 10th, the Soviet Don Front launched operation *Koltso* ("*Ring*"), with a barrage from 7,000 guns and heavy VVS bombing and ground attack raids. Rokossovsky selected the weakly defended western side of the pocket for the assault and Paulus was soon driven back to the Rossoshka River.

The 16th Air Army, now 525 aircraft strong with 215 fighters, 103 Shturmoviks, 105 day bombers, 87 night bombers, 15 reconnaissance, and 75 liaison and transport aircraft, supported *Koltso* with 676 sorties on the 10th and claimed 14 aerial victories in 25 air engagements. Only a few Bf 109s and three Stukas remained at Pitomnik, although they claimed eight enemy aircraft destroyed on the day of the offensive. The 16th VA maintained

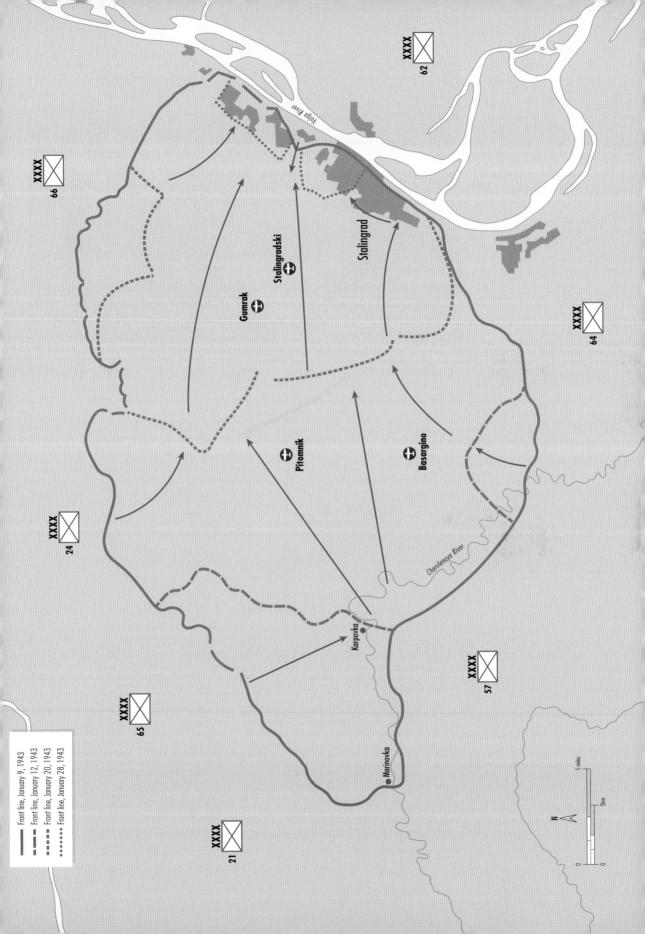

Front line, January 9, 1943
Front line, January 12, 1943
Front line, January 20, 1943
Front line, January 28, 1943

XXXX
62

XXXX
66

XXXX
64

XXXX
24

XXXX
57

XXXX
65

XXXX
21

Volga River

Stalingradski

Gumrak

Stalingrad

Pitomnik

Basargino

Chervlenaya River

Karpovka

Marinovka

N

5 miles
5km

Generalfeldmarschall von Paulus in Soviet captivity. Paulus and his forces in a pocket in the southern portion of the city capitulated on January 30; the Luftwaffe tried to drop supplies to forces holding out in the northern factory portion until their collapse three days later. (Courtesy of the Central Museum of the Armed Forces, Moscow, via Stavka)

the pressure with 900 sorties against the Sixth Army on the 11th and 12th. Having won almost complete air superiority over the pocket, the Soviets began to launch rare daylight operations by Long-Range Aviation bombers and its 3, 17, 53, and 62 Aviation Divisions bombed German positions on January 12, at times employing heavy FAB-250 and FAB-500 bombs. The few German Pitomnik fighters remaining were only able to engage and damage a small number of bombers.

The Luftwaffe strained to aid the beleaguered defenders from outside the pocket. On January 13, Bomber Group 51 dispatched its Ju 88s to Stalingrad to bomb in support of the Sixth Army, and 69 transports reached Pitomnik that night. The few remaining Bf 109s fought on, claiming 17 VVS aircraft shot down on the 15th. Two Bf 109s were dispatched on a one-way escort mission to reinforce the base, but the lead Bf 109 pilot reported back that Pitomnik was littered with wrecks and unburied corpses and the ground situation was chaotic. Soviet artillery began to hit the field the same day, and operational fighters, Stukas, and reconnaissance aircraft evacuated to Gumrak, the only other major airfield in the pocket. Twelve Bf 109s were left behind as derelicts, and five were able to fly off – one strafing attacking Soviet infantry immediately after lifting off the runway – but Gumrak was in such poor condition that four were damaged attempting to land on the shell-hole-filled runway. The Sixth Army had resisted all Luftwaffe efforts to improve Gumrak throughout the siege, as the army and two corps headquarters and hospital facilities were located nearby and army command did not want to attract Soviet attention. As a result, on the 16th the field lacked signals and radio beacons and the runway was cratered.

Paulus ordered Pickert to fly out of the pocket and make clear the plight of the Sixth Army to Berlin. Pickert met with Luftwaffe senior leadership, but a planned briefing to Hitler was waved off at the last minute. Pickert insisted on returning to his men, but as his He 111 circled Pitomnik at 0100 hours on January 16, it was unable to identify the normal radio signal or pick up the landing lights. Soviet ground forces were overrunning the airfield that same night, leaving the Sixth Army only the ill-prepared field at Gumrak. Pickert returned to Taganrog and was ultimately given command of the Flak defenses of the Army Group A forces retreating to the Kuban Peninsula opposite Crimea.

While crushing the pocket, the Soviets continued to hammer the German front to the west. Again targeting portions of the front held by weaker Axis allied forces, the Voronezh Front launched an offensive against the Second Hungarian Army's positions on the Don on

January 12. The attacking forces were supported by General-Mayor Konstantin Smirnov's 2nd Air Army, now over 500 aircraft including 200 fighters and 200 Il-2s. Richthofen had posted *Luftwaffencommando* (Air Command) Don to support Army Group B, while the VIII Air Corps concentrated on the airlift with the bulk of the 4th Air Fleet's forces. Air Command Don only contained a single fighter group and small numbers of bombers and Stukas and was heavily outnumbered. As with the first hours of *Uranus* and *Little Saturn*, however, poor weather on the 12th limited air operations, with Smirnov's pilots only managing 84 combat sorties, 39 of them at night. Despite the limited air support, the Voronezh Front rapidly shattered the Hungarian defenses and began exploitation attacks to the west and southwest, further imperiling the entire German front.

Forced to evacuate Salsk on January 16, the Ju 52s shifted to the newly constructed base at Zverevo. The Ju 52s were parked closely together on the narrowly plowed section of the runway, and eight waves of five to seven VVS aircraft were able to damage over 50 of the transports on the 17th and destroy 12 the next day. Stocks of supplies were also destroyed in the attack. Fritz Morzik, at last assigned to the airlift and commanding at Zverevo, reported that the Rumanian Flak gunners fled, but the one German-manned 37mm position downed one of the attacking Il-2s.

Milch on the scene

At last focusing on the airlift, Hitler dispatched Generalfeldmarschall Erhard Milch – the Luftwaffe's deputy supreme commander and inspector general – to improve the situation. Milch was given special authority over all services and assets in the area. The field marshal received briefings about the actual condition of the 4th Air Fleet at Richthofen's headquarters at Taganrog, something not fully understood at high command levels. General Weidinger, the air fleet chief engineer, gave a snapshot of transport readiness on January 16: 41 of 140 He 111s and 15 of 140 Ju 52s at the airfields were able to fly – readiness rates of only 29 and 11 percent. None of the fragile Fw 200s was serviceable. Only seven Ju 52s and 11 He 111s were being prepared to fly supplies to the pocket that night. Prospects to improve aircraft readiness were grim, and Weidinger stated it would take two weeks to improve it by 50 percent. The impact of VVS operations was brought home with reports that bombing raids on Zverevo had destroyed nine aircraft and left 12 damaged, leaving only 12 Ju 52s operational. Determined to visit the airfields and assess conditions for himself, Milch set off

German prisoners of war. Weakened by poor rations, freezing weather, and disease, most of the 91,000 prisoners taken at Stalingrad rapidly died and only 6,000 were alive to be released in the 1950s. (Courtesy of the Central Museum of the Armed Forces, Moscow, via Stavka)

Built for swift, successful campaigns, the Luftwaffe lacked a permanent air transport force and had to draw Ju 52s from its training establishment when needed. For Stalingrad, the size of the effort led to many additional, ill-prepared aircraft being requisitioned from the government, Lufthansa, and the post office. (Nik Cornish at www.Stavka.org.uk)

on the 17th to start at Taganrog Airfield, but his car was struck at a railroad crossing by a train emerging suddenly from the morning fog, leaving him with head injuries and a plaster cast around his back and ribs.

Undaunted, Milch checked himself out of the hospital and worked intensely to improve the situation from the 4th's headquarters. Rather than alter the current command arrangements, Milch established a small *Sonderstab* (special staff) consisting of a few officers, advisors, and signals personnel to assist the airlift. Milch quickly realized that critical reinforcements, supplies, and personnel were "stuck" in the cumbersome and overwhelmed logistical pipeline stretching back to the Reich and made efforts, including threats of court martial, to get what was needed moving to the front.

The transport force was at an all-time high in numbers when Milch arrived – 690 in total, with 368 Ju 52s, 272 He 11s, 22 Fw 200s and 28 He 177s – but poor maintenance and logistical support was crippling readiness. Of the 690, 316 were actually in place on the airfields, and of these, only 61 were operational on January 17. Milch immediately ordered additional ground crews and maintenance equipment, including more of the critical warming vehicles, to be dispatched from Germany, and backed the creation of new workshops behind the front so that aircraft did not have to be sent all the way back to Germany for repair. Milch discovered that many Ju 52 crews were not using the proper cold start procedures. Many of them had been operating in Africa or the Balkans, and others had been taken from postal, courier, or Lufthansa duties. Milch imported 50 experts from the Luftwaffe testing and development base at Rechlin to supervise additional training in the proper way to start up the Ju 52s even in freezing conditions, but reports continued that crews were backsliding. Eventually Milch threatened any crew not using the proper procedures with court martial.

Milch's initiatives were needed, but he arrived too late for most to have an appreciable impact. Due to the limited capacity of the rail net, the majority of the additional maintenance personnel and equipment only arrived at the front after the Sixth Army had surrendered, as did the 13,000 250kg and 7,000 1,000kg supply containers for airdrops he ordered produced.

To improve fighter cover for transports flying from the more distant airfields at Novocherkassk and Zverevo, Milch ordered drop tanks and long-range Bf 110 fighters be sent to the front, but only nine long-range Bf 109Gs and five Bf 110s reached the front on January 27, only a week before the final surrender in the pocket. They were few in number, and the Bf 110s fitted with the long-range fuel tanks were C-1 models rather than the more capable Fs requested. Milch insisted the five Bf 110s and six of the Bf 109s using the fuel tanks fly over Stalingrad on January 30 in a symbolic, if hollow, operation to mark the tenth anniversary of Hitler's accession to power.

Some of Milch's initiatives proved even less useful. He was determined to use gliders to increase supply deliveries, an idea already considered and rejected by the 4th Air Fleet. Gliders were more vulnerable to poor weather and could not be used in strong winds. The Germans lacked long-range fighters to adequately cover their Ju 52s, and certainly could not protect vulnerable gliders. The collapsing pocket had no facilities to receive the gliders, and if they landed in fields the Sixth Army lacked the fuel to recover, unload, and distribute any supplies. Milch was insistent, however, and for some time every third day a train arrived loaded with gliders – a waste of valuable rail capacity. By the 25th it was clear that there was no potential to employ them, and Milch admitted defeat and transferred the gliders to the south where they could be used in support of Army Group A.

Milch and the airfields

A major challenge was the poor state of Gumrak. Paulus insisted the airfield was fully ready to receive supply flights, but five He 111s that arrived on the 17th reported no ground crews to unload the cargo or control the crowds that tried to storm the planes. Milch sent in a team of officers and personnel to determine the condition of the field, rapidly followed by equipment and signals personnel to ready it for night landings. Milch assured Paulus that supplies would be landed on the night of the 18th, and an Fw 200 Condor carrying six tons along with six He 111s were able to land thanks to the radio beacon, direction finder equipment, and an improvised system of lights formed by ten tanks illuminating the landing path that had been set up. The Luftwaffe sustained flights over the next several days, but at a cost. Turnaround times for aircraft landing at Gumrak was five hours, and the airfield remained pockmarked by craters from Soviet artillery fire. About a fourth of all the He 111s crashed or were damaged landing or taking off from the field.

Soviet forces overran Gumrak on January 23. Some effort had been made to prepare the airfield of Stalingradskiy to receive landings if Gumrak was lost, but several He 111s attempting to land there crashed or were damaged due to snow and bomb craters on the runway. Milch directed that only He 111s could try to use the field, and only in daylight hours. The last He 111 took off from Stalingradskiy late on January 23 carrying 19 wounded soldiers and seven bags of mail, just before that airfield too was overrun by Soviet forces.

Il-2 Shturmovik strafe and bomb Zverevo Airfield, January 17, 1943

The Luftwaffe had to withdraw its Ju 52s from Salsk to the newly constructed airfield at Zverevo on January 16. Zverevo had been rapidly built in a frozen cornfield and had no hangars or infrastructure. The arriving Ju 52s had to be closely parked on the narrow plowed portions of the runway. On January 17 and 18, the VVS launched a series of airstrikes on the airfield. Eight waves of five to seven attackers came in on the 17th, opposed by only a single 37mm anti-aircraft position manned by German personnel. Base commander Oberst Morzik reported that Rumanian troops assigned to a 75mm AAA battery took shelter in trenches during the attacks. The base took heavy losses, and a total of 50 transports were damaged and 12 completely destroyed over the two days of raids.

He 111s at a snowy airfield. Weather conditions had a major impact on Luftwaffe aviation operations. Planes were difficult to de-ice and warm due to sub-zero temperatures and a lack of equipment. (Nik Cornish at www.Stavka.org.uk)

The Luftwaffe could now only supply the Sixth Army through airdrops. Purpose-built containers helped the process, but lacking these some crews simply pushed crates out the door. The Sixth Army's lack of fuel made the recovery and distribution of these supplies difficult.

Paulus' defense was now in tatters. The 16th Air Army had complete air superiority over the remnants of the pocket and, augmented by the bombers of Long-Range Aviation, struck targets at will. The Soviets drove to the Volga River on the 26th, dividing the defenders into two pockets. The remnants of the XI Corps under General Kurt Strecker held the northern factory area of Stalingrad, while the remainder of the army defended the city's southern districts. The condition of the troops was dire, and two days later the Sixth Army stopped issuing rations to the 25,000 wounded, hoping to keep the few able troops fighting as long as possible. Paulus requested that only food supplies be airdropped.

Richthofen and Fiebig resolved to make every effort to drop supplies to the pockets but initially were uncertain where to make the drops. Major Freudenfeld, the senior Luftwaffe signals officer with the Sixth Army, mobilized troops to clear and mark drop zones in the southern pocket. He installed radio beacons and had truck headlights used to mark the zone for night drops. After establishing the southern zone on the 25th, he was able to set up a similar one in the northern zone three days later. By the 30th, the southern pocket was on the verge of collapse and Milch ordered that supply drops be focused on the northern pocket. Eighty-five aircraft departed that night, although 30 had to turn back due to weather or mechanical problems, but the 55 that got through dropped 72 tons. They were unable to identify German positions and drop zones to the south. That morning, Freudenfeld signaled that Soviet troops were at the door and signed off; Paulus surrendered with 11 German and Rumanian general officers several hours later.

Strecker's troops continued fighting, and the Luftwaffe dispatched another lift of 85 transports that dropped 74 tons on the night of January 31/February 1. Signal lamps and a defiant swastika outlined with red lights in the snow indicated some positions were still resisting. The next evening 116 Ju 52s dropped 98 tons, but it is uncertain if much was retrieved by the remaining combatants. Strecker signaled his surrender on the 2nd. The Luftwaffe flew aircraft over Stalingrad that night, but no fighting positions were visible, and the next day Milch ordered the stand-down of the airlift organization.

AFTERMATH AND ASSESSMENT

As Paulus and his men marched into captivity, attrition had reduced Richthofen's 4th Air Fleet to 642 combat aircraft, 240 of which were operational. The 4th still had a large force of 477 transports, mostly Ju 52s but also three He 111 groups. On January 31, only 30 percent of these were able to fly – about 146 transports. The He 111 bombers had suffered from operating on poor runways, and their readiness was particularly low. Of the 55th Wing's 52 surviving He 111s, only 12 were flyable at the end of the month, and 18 of the 66 He 111s in the 27th Wing. Morale and effectiveness of the ground personnel had suffered due to the long months of work without relief in freezing weather, VVS raids on the bases, and the frequent need to evacuate bases under pressure of Soviet ground attack.

There would be no easing of the demands on the 4th Air Fleet. Army Group A had withdrawn from its forward positions in the Caucasus, with the First Panzer Army moving toward Rostov and the Seventeenth Army ordered by Hitler to hold the Kuban Peninsula and maintain a threat to the Caucasus. Manstein needed Richthofen's support as he withdrew into the Donbas region of Ukraine. The 4th Air Fleet was also tasked with supplying the forces in the Kuban by air until they could be supplied by sea in the spring. Richthofen's forces at least benefited from being able to fall back on better supplied and more secure airbases in Crimea and Ukraine, while the Soviets advanced at the end of a lengthening line of communications.

Feibig's VIII Air Corps assumed responsibility for support to the Kuban, and its newly formed *Luftransporteinsatz Krim* (Air Transport Mission Crimea) immediately began operations from its new bases. Fiebig retained all its ground maintenance personnel and equipment but reorganized its ten heavily attritted and low readiness transport groups into five with 180 operational aircraft. All aircraft needing repair were sent to the rear. The well-equipped airfield network and arrival of the supplies Milch had ordered for Stalingrad allowed the transports to maintain a 60–75 percent readiness rate and fly an average of

A Soviet Il-4 medium bomber being towed into position by ground support equipment. While the VVS reported ammunition and fuel shortfalls before the launching of Operation *Uranus*, its forces were much more prepared for sustaining operations in the harsh winter weather typical of the southern USSR. (Courtesy of the Central Museum of the Armed Forces, Moscow, via Stavka)

Летчику Сталинградского фронта
Гвардии Майору тов. Еремину "Стахановец"
От колхозника колхоза тов. Головатова.

While Luftwaffe officers were quick to blame the weather for the airlift's failure, the VVS had won the USSR its first strategic victory in the air. Many VVS air blockade pilots were able to gain ace status. Guards Major Yeremin is pictured after his seventh victory; his plane carries a dedication from a collective farm that sponsored his fighter. (Photo by Sovfoto/ Universal Images Group via Getty Images)

182 tons of supplies to the Seventeenth Army bridgehead daily. This was well above the average amount managed by the Stalingrad airlift, with only a fraction of the number of transports. The airlift allowed the Seventeeth Army to sustain its defense until the spring weather allowed supply by sea.

Richthofen's reorganized 4th Air Fleet played a major role in Manstein's famous "backhand blow" counteroffensive in the Kharkov area. Like the Luftwaffe, Manstein's Army Group Don forces – now merged with Army Group B and redesignated Army Group South – gained strength as it fell back on its bases and a stronger logistics infrastructure, while attacking Soviet forces were overextended and 200 miles from their supply sources. Richthofen shifted his headquarters from Mariupol to Zaporozhye in mid-February to work more closely with Manstein and assigned Pflugbeil's IV Air Corps to support operations around Kharkov. Richthofen's aircraft played a vital role aiding the attacking panzers as they encircled the stalled Soviet armored spearheads. The 4th Air Fleet was able to increase its sortie rates from an average of about 350 a day in January to 1,000 during Manstein's offensive. Richthofen's energy and command style played a major role in the success, as he flew in his Storch from headquarters to headquarters to animate his Luftwaffe units and plan air strikes in concert with various ground force commanders. Unlike during the last few months, the Germans again had the initiative, and the panzers and Luftwaffe could mass their combat power on key targets and axes of advance. The Army Group South counterattack began on February 20 and Kharkov was retaken on March 15. German forces had restored the line from which they launched Operation *Blau* nine months before.

The Stalingrad airlift: an assessment

Despite the success at Kharkov, the Axis had suffered a devastating defeat. Apart from the wounded and small numbers of specialist personnel evacuated by air, the 22 divisions of the Sixth Army were completely destroyed. From a force of over a quarter of a million troops, only 91,000 survived to be taken prisoner. Four other Axis armies – the Third and Fourth Rumanian, Eighth Italian and Second Hungarian – had been destroyed by a series of Soviet offensives along the line of the Don, and the Germans would never rely on their allies to hold sectors of the front again. In all, over half a million Axis troops had been lost. The gains of Operation *Blau* had been wiped out, and German forces were fortunate to stabilize the front basically on the same line they had held in June, 1942. As Paulus and the remnants of his once proud army surrendered in the ruins of Stalingrad, the Axis faced a series of defeats across the globe from North Africa to the Pacific, and it soon became clear that the tide of the war had decisively turned in the Allies' favor.

Tonnage delivered	Days of airlift achieved	Percentage of 71-day airlift
0–50	13	19
51–100	23	32
101–150	18	25
151–200	5	7
201–250	5	7
251–300	3	4
301 +	4	5

The Luftwaffe's effort to supply the Sixth Army had failed, as its frontline leaders had predicted from the first. A total of 4,487 transport sorties had landed in or dropped supplies to the pocket, delivering just over 8,300 metric tons over the 71 days of the airlift – an average of 117 tons delivered each day. This amounted to only a third of the minimum 300 needed to keep the army in being, and a fraction of the 500 and 750 tons that staffs assessed were needed to keep the army fully effective. The magnitude of the Luftwaffe's shortfall is striking. No transports at all arrived in the pocket for four of the airlift's 71 days, three due to severe weather, and on Christmas Day due to the Soviet tank raids against Tatsinskaya and Morozovsk. On nine other days, the airlift delivered less than 50 tons of supplies. Only on

A Shturmovik pilot congratulates his rear gunner. Il-2 Shturmoviks were heavily armored to protect the engine and cockpit against ground fire but were vulnerable to German fighter attack from above and behind. VVS units began to install improvised rear gunner positions in their Shturmoviks, and during the Stalingrad campaign increasing numbers of Il-2Ms with rear gunner positions began to reach the front, increasing the survivability of the USSR's premier attack plane. (Courtesy of the Central Museum of the Armed Forces, Moscow, via Stavka)

four days was the Sixth Army's minimal 300-ton requirement met. Transport arrival statistics parallel the tonnage numbers, with the 4th Air Fleet only getting over 100 transports through to the pocket on 15 days. The delivery of the 300-ton daily requirement would have given the Sixth Army 21,300 tons; the actual delivery of 8,300 meant a 13,000 shortfall for the troops isolated in the pocket.

Number of aircraft arriving at pocket	Number of days achieved	Percentage of 71-day airlift
0–50	24	33
51–100	33	46
101–150	14	19
151–200	1	2

Given that the Sixth Army had already been operating on a logistical shoestring when encircled, its deterioration was rapid. Fuel and ammunition were the priority for the first five weeks, but the supplies delivered by the Luftwaffe did not even cover daily requirements. When Manstein's *Winter Storm* force closed to within 30 miles of the Stalingrad perimeter, the Sixth Army reported it only had fuel to move 20 miles, and any opportunity to launch a breakout passed. Even if it had been attempted, the lack of fuel meant leaving the wounded and large amounts of artillery and equipment behind. As any prospect for a breakout ended in late December, it became clear that the Sixth Army's most critical need was rations, and food and medical supplies comprised the bulk of deliveries in January. The flights never approached the estimated 255 tons of food needed daily to keep the troops adequately fed, and the reductions in rations that were instituted as early as November had a steady negative impact on the health and morale of the soldiers. Malnourished, frozen, and short of ammunition and fuel, the Sixth Army was unable to hold off the Soviet Operation *Koltso* offensive in January. The 91,000 prisoners taken were so weak from starvation and disease that only 6,000 or so survived the harsh conditions of their captivity to return to Germany in the 1950s. While unable to adequately supply the pocket, returning Luftwaffe transports did succeed in evacuating 24,700 wounded and 5,150 other personnel.

VVS Pe-2 light bombers. In addition to the famous Il-2 Shturmoviks, the VVS used Pe-2s, B-3 Bostons, and Il-4s extensively both to strike Luftwaffe airfields and support ground attacks by Red Army forces driving Army Group Don back toward Rostov. (Courtesy of the Central Museum of the Armed Forces, Moscow, via Stavka)

The Luftwaffe's efforts were costly in addition to being unsuccessful. Milch's staff tallied the losses as 488 transports overall, with 274 destroyed or missing and 214 damaged so badly they had to be written off as losses. Of these 266 were Ju 52s, amounting to over a third of the Luftwaffe's total force. Also lost were 165 He 111 bombers being used in the transport role, as well as 42 Ju 86s, nine Fw 200 Condors, five of the developmental He 177 bombers, and one Ju 290 airliner. Given the total of 6,098 sorties that took off for the pocket, the German loss estimates would give an overall loss rate from all causes of over eight percent. Over 1,000 pilots and aircrew – many experts drawn from the training establishment – were killed in action. Soviet sources claim over 900 transports were destroyed, almost certainly an exaggerated total, but may include some aircraft destroyed or abandoned at bases that are not included in Milch's totals.

Luftwaffe challenges

From the day Milch shut down the airlift operation on February 3, various causes for its failure have been put forth, most pointing to the weather or a lack of transport aircraft. In reality, the Luftwaffe faced numerous challenges as it struggled to supply the Sixth Army. At the very top, German leadership and command and control were troubled. Having announced the Luftwaffe could do the job and contributed his own VIP transport to the effort, Göring left for Paris and never gave the operation the top-level attention and support it needed. Lacking Göring's backing and consumed with combat operations at the front, the 4th Air Fleet was unable to overcome the administrative constraints and bureaucratic hurdles that crippled its efforts to obtain vitally needed supplies, maintenance personnel, and spare parts. Only when Hitler sent Milch, fully empowered to cut through the red tape and get things moving, was some progress made, but his arrival was far too late. As he stepped off the plane at Taganrog, the airfield at Pitomnik was being overrun by Rokossovsky's troops, and the final surrender of the pocket was less than three weeks away.

At the front, the 4th Air Fleet's leadership of the airlift was energetic but uneven. Oberst Morzik, the leader of the Demyansk operation and the Luftwaffe's leading expert on airlift operations, was not employed or even consulted as the airlift got underway and was only assigned there in January. General Victor Carganico was initially assigned to lead the effort but proved a failure, and within days Richthofen replaced him with Fiebig and the VIII Air Corps staff, who brought combat expertise but lacked experience in running a supply air bridge. In the pocket, 9th Flak Division commander Pickert was capable and energetic but lacked the seniority and authority needed to work with the Sixth Army staff on an equal basis and was unable to overcome the Sixth Army's resistance to preparing Gumrak for operations. Paulus and his staff showed little interest in working closely with the Luftwaffe to improve the supply operation and focused primarily on increasingly desperate complaints to Berlin that the air force was letting them down.

The quality of the transport force also posed difficulties. The Luftwaffe lacked a large, permanent transport organization and had to rely on a hastily assembled, ad hoc assembly of transports, many unprepared for the rigors of combat operations during the Russian winter. About 250 of the Luftwaffe's 750 Ju 52s were dedicated to operations in North Africa, and to build up the Stalingrad force more transports were drawn from a wide variety of sources, ranging from the Lufthansa to the post office. Aircraft and personnel were of mixed quality, with some of the planes nearing the end of their service lives. Pressure from above to rapidly build up the force in the USSR led the preparation centers in Ukraine to take many shortcuts, and many of the civilian and even some of the military Ju 52s arrived without the insulation, communications, and defensive upgrades they needed.

In the air, the Ju 52s were vulnerable to Soviet fighters and even Il-2 Shturmoviks due to their slow cruising speed. The Luftwaffe's He 111s proved to be very useful in

A well-camouflaged VVS bomber receiving maintenance at its base. The Soviets placed a great emphasis on *maskirovka*, the use of camouflage, concealment, and deception as a force multiplier during military operations. As part of his preparations for *Uranus*, VVS Commander-in-Chief Novikov directed the preparation of 19 dummy airfields along with large numbers of operational airfields east of the Volga. (Courtesy of the Central Museum of the Armed Forces, Moscow, via Stavka)

the transport role, with better speed and a stronger defensive armament. He 111 crews were typically better prepared to fly in combat conditions and in poor weather or at night and completed 2,577 sorties while the Ju 52s flew 2,139. The bombers' impact was limited by their smaller tonnage capacity, about half that of the Ju 52, and their frequent diversion to their primary role as bombers to support the *Winter Storm* attack and counter Soviet attacks. The other types sent to augment the airlift only appeared in small numbers and made a limited contribution. The two groups of Ju 86s had many shortfalls, could only carry 800kg of supplies, and only performed 74 sorties, while losing 42 of their number to maintenance, weather, and enemy action. In January, the Luftwaffe sent high-capacity Fw 200 and two Ju 290 aircraft to the effort, but these were difficult to maintain and suffered heavy losses. The troubled developmental He 177 bomber made almost no contribution, with 17 sorties bringing in about 19 tons of supplies at the cost of five aircraft.

The airlift lacked a network of well-supplied, equipped, and secure airfields. Even if Hitler had augmented the Stalingrad lift with the 250 Ju 52s dedicated to supporting the airlift to Tunisia, the basing and support infrastructure would have been unable to support them. The few underequipped airfields available were unable to adequately support the hundreds of transport aircraft, widely varying in equipment and readiness when they arrived. Maintenance personnel and equipment, especially the vital *Warmewagen* vehicles used to warm and start engines in cold weather, were in short supply, as were spare parts for the Ju 52s. Winter weather made ground support operations even more difficult, with personnel typically having to dig out bombers from snowdrifts in the morning and clear runways often with hand tools. Tatsinskaya and Morozovsk had some hangars and barracks but were inadequate to support all the needed maintenance operations, and many had to be performed by ground crews in the open, freezing weather. The situation at other airfields, especially the primitive and hastily constructed field at Zverevo, was even worse. The loss of maintenance personnel and equipment began as the Luftwaffe's forward airfields were overrun by the *Uranus* offensive and worsened with the loss of Tatsinskaya and Morozovsk in late December. Morzik assessed that the Airfield Servicing Companies that were able to escape from those fields were only able to operate at 35–45 percent capacity in January.

The impact on transport operational readiness rates was profound. The Luftwaffe was able to expand the total number of transports from under 200 in late November to over 400 by early December and over 600 by mid-January, but a third to one-half were constantly in transit or receiving depot maintenance in rear areas. Of those at the forward airfields, only a portion could be made ready to fly each day, and the average number of transports

Loading tins into a supply drop canister. Ammunition and fuel were the priority during the first weeks of the airlift, but when prospects for a successful relief faded, most supplies flown in by the Luftwaffe were food and medical supplies. (Nik Cornish at www.Stavka.org.uk)

operational daily throughout the airlift was 92, with an average of 68 landing in the pocket. As the table below outlines, the arrival of additional transports in January had little impact on the overall percentage that could be kept operational given the logistical and maintenance challenges faced by the Luftwaffe. The average readiness for the entire 71-day airlift was 21 percent.

Dates	Average number of transports assigned to 4th Air Fleet	Average number at forward airfields	Average number of operational aircraft	Average arrivals in pocket	Total supplies delivered (tons)	Average daily deliveries of supplies (tons)
Nov 24–30	222	117	61	43	526	75
Dec 1–11	389	259	137	63	1,443	131
Dec 12–31	425	243	96	73	2,767	138
Jan 1–15	487	252	72	73	2,257	150
Jan 16– Feb 3	571	338	84	71	1,323	70
Total average for airlift: 24 Nov, 1942–3 Feb, 1943.	451	260	92	68	8,316	115

German officers during and after the war stressed that weather conditions rather than Soviet opposition were the major factor frustrating the airlift. The winter weather made maintenance of the aircraft and warming the engines each day extremely difficult. Transports in the air faced sudden snowstorms and icing, and large numbers were unable to reach the pocket or were reported lost in flight due to weather issues. While specific numbers are lacking, Luftwaffe officers ascribed about half of the transport losses to weather, either lost in flight or damaged while trying to take off or land. Weather prohibited any German aircraft from reaching the pocket on December 3 and 9 and January 2. Good, clear flying weather was not always desirable, however, and after mid-December the Luftwaffe would only fly in daylight if there were enough clouds or fog to provide cover from the VVS "free hunter" fighters. Operations were canceled from Salsk on seven out of nine days in early January when the weather forecasts indicated inadequate clouds for cover.

The Soviet air effort

Despite Luftwaffe officers at the time and after the war downplaying its impact, the VVS won the air battle for Stalingrad as much as the Luftwaffe lost it. The Germans lost air superiority after *Uranus*, and the airlift had to be executed in the face of effective Soviet opposition in the air and frequent raids on German airfields both inside and outside the pocket. The Soviet airmen not only frustrated the efforts of the 4th Air Fleet to supply Stalingrad but at the same time provided powerful support to the Red Army as it launched *Uranus*, defeated the *Winter Storm* relief, and conducted a series of offensives that destroyed the Eighth Italian and Second Hungarian Armies and ultimately drove the Wehrmacht back into the Ukraine.

Soviet leadership was an advantage. While Göring absented himself from day-to-day management of the airlift, VVS Commander-in-Chief Novikov had been on the scene since late August, serving as the Stavka aviation representative and coordinating the actions of the air armies, 102nd PVO Division, and bombers of Long-Range Aviation. Soviet air power was no longer shackled to ground armies, and Novikov was able to wield his forces effectively using the new air army organization. This flexibility allowed Novikov to rapidly shift the Eighth, Sixteenth, and Seventeenth Armies between different tasks in mid-December to help blunt the LVII Panzer Corps relief attempt, maintain the air blockade, and support offensive operations against the Italian Eighth Army.

The VVS also demonstrated improvements on the tactical level. Soviet pilots were now able to engage their foes using the *para-zveno* four- and two-plane formations rather than the rigid and vulnerable three-plane *Katte*. More and more VVS aircraft had full radio sets, and the radio control network established just behind the front line proved adept at guiding Soviet pilots to their targets. Elite units such as the 9th Guards' "ace regiment" helped engender a new aggressive spirit in the VVS.

A key factor in the VVS's success at Stalingrad was the employment of its Il-2 Shturmovik force. For the first time, Shturmoviks were employed in large numbers, with 575 available at the start of *Uranus* in late November. The Il-2 pilots employed improved tactics learned at high cost during the first year of the war, including shallow dives to increase accuracy. Armored against ground fire but vulnerable to fighter attacks from the behind, the Shturmoviks also took measures to improve their defensive capabilities, at first with improvised rear gunner positions and later with factory-produced models. The Pe-2 bomber force also began to favor the use of dive-bombing techniques to improve accuracy. The Il-2s and bombers both continually supported Red Army operations on the ground and conducted frequent raids on the key Luftwaffe air bases during the campaign.

While successful, the cost in aircraft and aircrew remained high. While claims of aerial victories by both sides are exaggerated, the Luftwaffe was likely able to bring down at least three Soviet aircraft for each one it lost, and its aces added numerous victories to their tallies. The VVS continued to push pilots and aircrew with minimal training into the front line, and these fresh pilots were easy victims for the German veterans. During the campaign one Luftwaffe fighter wing claimed its 4,000th victory; even if exaggerated, the total losses inflicted by this unit and many others were clearly very high. But, while the VVS lost aircraft and aircrew in large numbers, the USSR was able to keep its units up to strength. Aviation factories had been safely evacuated to the Urals and were producing at high capacity in

The failed airlift to Stalingrad was preceded and followed by successful aerial resupply of German forces at Demyansk and the Kuban due to better equipped and more secure airbases and more limited VVS opposition. (Nik Cornish at www. Stavka.org.uk)

1942, and the Soviets produced 25,436 aircraft during the year. Germany only produced 15,596, and the Luftwaffe would need to use many of these to defend the Reich against the Allied combined bombing offensive and for other theaters. The staying power of the VVS was reflected in its high operational rate – 35,920 sorties by Soviet aircraft during the Stalingrad counteroffensive phase (November 19, 1942 to February 3, 1943), as against around 18,500 German.

While the VVS battled the Luftwaffe to a standstill in the air, the revitalized Soviet army played the decisive role in defeating Axis forces in the southern USSR. The German summer offensive had left the Sixth Army in a precarious position at the end of a long salient into enemy territory with weak forces protecting its flanks. Hitler was hopeful in November, 1942 that the Soviets were weakening, but the next months proved the opposite to be true. As with its air arm, the USSR was able to replace losses in its ground forces and dispatch unit after unit of fresh infantry, armor, and artillery to the front. The Red Army's subsequent winter offensives encircled Paulus in Stalingrad, held and drove back Manstein's *Winter Storm* attack, and destroyed the Eighth Italian and Second Hungarian Armies. Simultaneously, the Stavka was able to assemble enough combat power to launch the offensive that forced the final capitulation of the Sixth Army on February 2. Ultimately, Axis forces were driven back to their June, 1942 start line with crippling strategic losses.

The Red Army advances also posed direct threats to the Luftwaffe's network of airlift bases. The *Little Saturn* offensive broke through Axis lines and enabled two tank corps to move to threaten the critical airlift bases at Tatsinskaya and Morozovsk. The 24th Tank Corps inflicted heavy losses on the massed Ju 52 transport force at the former, and although the 25th never reached the latter, both airfields had to be evacuated by late December, driving the Luftwaffe to inferior bases much farther from the pocket. The Ju 52s were only able to operate from their new location at Salsk for less than three weeks before being driven by Soviet ground forces yet again further west. Arriving at the improvised Ju 52 base hastily plowed out of the frozen earth at Zverevo, the Germans found themselves forced to use the poorest airfield employed during the entire campaign.

The Luftwaffe's failure at Stalingrad was preceded by the successful airlift to Demyansk and followed by successful support of the Kuban bridgehead. All three airlifts faced difficult weather conditions, but at Demyansk and the Kuban the Luftwaffe was able to base its lift from better-equipped and more secure airbases, while its airfields during Stalingrad were undersupplied, overcrowded, and constantly threatened by Red Army advances. Further, the VVS mounted its strongest effort at Stalingrad. At Demyansk, the Soviet airmen were slow to concentrate against the airlift and had not benefited from Novikov's leadership and reforms, as reflected in the 106 transports lost, half to weather and half to Soviet action. Over the Kuban, the strain of the Stalingrad operation and the need to restore its forces and logistics limited the VVS's ability to challenge the Luftwaffe airlift in the first months of 1943. In contrast, the VVS air blockade of Stalingrad crippled the Luftwaffe's efforts through constant raids on its bases, an effective anti-aircraft effort, and interceptor zones that forced the Germans to switch to avoid clear weather daylight fights. The demands on Richthofen's limited numbers of fighters, Stukas, and bombers were so intense that it could never spare assets to strike Soviet anti-aircraft positions or airfields or even successfully escort its transport flights.

The Stalingrad campaign and the Luftwaffe's failed airlift marked the moment when the German war machine, built for short, decisive, and successful offensives, was decisively defeated by an opponent willing to engage in a costly and protracted campaign of attrition. The Luftwaffe would still be able to mass its forces and challenge the VVS for the next few years, but Novikov's airmen were on the path that would lead to Shturmoviks flying over the ruins of Berlin two years later.

FURTHER READING

While the overall trends are consistent, there is some variation in the daily numbers and statistics for sorties and tons of supplies delivered given in different sources for the Stalingrad airlift. For consistency I have relied in this account on the comprehensive statistical tables in Manfred Kehrig's *Stalingrad: Analyze und Dokumentation einer Schlacht*, 1974.

For an excellent account of the Luftwaffe campaign in the east in 1942, with a particular focus on the Stalingrad airlift, see the comprehensive *Stopped at Stalingrad: The Luftwaffe and Hitler's Defeat in the East 1942–1943*, by Joel S. A. Hayward. Hayward focuses on the actions of the Luftwaffe commanders at the front and argues that more transports drawn from Africa would have improved the chances of a successful airlift. Aaron Bates argues persuasively in "For Want of the Means: A Logistical Appraisal of the Stalingrad Airlift," in *The Journal of Slavic Military Studies* that the Luftwaffe was unable to support the aircraft it did receive due to its poor logistical infrastructure, and it would have been unable to effectively employ additional reinforcements. Christer Bergstrom's *Stalingrad – The Air Battle: 1942 through January 1943* provides a detailed, day-by-day account of the air fighting in the south throughout the campaign and ascribes the failure of the airlift primarily to the efforts of the VVS.

Hermann Plocher wrote an analysis of Luftwaffe operations on the Eastern Front for the USAF after the war, as did Fritz Morzik on air transport issues. Richard Muller's *The German Air War in Russia*, 1999, addresses the broader German doctrinal and force planning issues surrounding its defeat at Stalingrad and on the Eastern Front in general. For the Soviet air effort, Von Hardesty's *Red Phoenix* covers VVS operations during the entire conflict and contains an in-depth discussion on Stalingrad. For the overall campaign, see the excellent studies by David Glantz.

Air operations in 1942 and the airlift

Bates, Aaron, "For Want of the Means: A Logistical Appraisal of the Stalingrad Airlift," in *The Journal of Slavic Military Studies,* Vol. 29 No. 2, 2016, pp. 298–318

Bekker, Cajus, *The Luftwaffe War Diaries: The German Air Force in World War II*, Da Capo Press: 1966

Bergstrom, Christer, *Stalingrad – The Air Battle: 1942 through January 1943*, Chevron Publishing: 2007

Forczyk, Robert, *Red Christmas: The Tatsinskaya Airfield Raid 1942*, Raid series, Osprey: 2012

Hayward, Joel A. S., *Stopped at Stalingrad: The Luftwaffe and Hitler's Defeat in the East 1942–1943*, University of Kansas Press, Lawrence: 1998

Kehrig, Manfred, *Stalingrad: Analyze und Dokumentation einer Schlacht*, Deutsche Verlags-Anstalt, Stuttgart: 1974

Morzik, Generalmajor D. Fritz, *German Air Force Airlift Operations*, edited by Edward P. Kennedy, USAF Historical Studies No. 167, USAF Historical Division, Research Studies Institute, Air University: 1961

Pickert, Wolfgang, "The Stalingrad Airlift: An Eyewitness Commentary," in *Aerospace Historian*, Vol. 18, No. 4, December 1971, pp. 183–185.

Plocher, Generalleutnant Hermann, *The German Air Force versus Russia, 1942*, edited by Harry Fletcher, USAF Historical Studies No. 154, USAF Historical Division, Research Studies Institute, Air University: 1966

Thyssen, Major Mike, *A Desperate Struggle to Save a Condemned Army – A Critical Review of the Stalingrad Airlift*, Air Command and Staff College, Maxwell Air Force Base, AL: 1997

The campaign

Forczyk, Robert, *Demyansk 1942–43: The Frozen Fortress*, Campaign series, Osprey: 2012

Forczyk, Robert, *Stalingrad 1942–43 (I): The German Advance to the Volga*, Campaign series, Osprey: 2021

Glantz, David M. and House, Jonathan M., *Endgame at Stalingrad, Book Two: December 1942–February 1943,* University Press of Kansas, Lawrence: 2014

Glantz, David M. and House, Jonathan M., *Stalingrad,* University Press of Kansas, Lawrence: 2017

Glantz, David M. and House, Jonathan M., *When Titans Clashed: How the Red Army Stopped Hitler (Revised and Expanded Edition)*, University Press of Kansas, Lawrence: 2015

Ziemke, Earl F. and Bauer, Magna E., *Moscow to Stalingrad: Decision in the East*, Military Heritage Press, New York: 1988

Ziemke, Earl F., *Stalingrad to Berlin: The German Defeat in the East*, Office of the Chief of Military History, United States Army, Washington, DC: 1968

The Luftwaffe and VVS

Hardesty, Von, and Grinberg, Ilya, *Red Phoenix Rising: The Soviet Air Force in World War II*, University of Kansas Press, Lawrence: 2012

Harvey, A. D., "The Russian Air Forces Against the Luftwaffe," in *Air Power History*, Vol. 65, No. 1, 2018, pp. 23–30

Kozhevnikov, M. N., *The Command and Staff of the Soviet Air Force in the Great Patriotic War, 1941–45: A Soviet View*, Moscow: 1977 (Translated and published under the auspices of the United States Air Force)

Kozhevnikov, M. and James L. Waddell, "Russian Aviation: Birth of the Air Armies," in *Aerospace Historian*, Vol. 22, No. 2, 1975, pp. 73–76 (Published by Air Force Historical Foundation)

Muller, Richard, *The German Air War in Russia*, The Nautical & Aviation Publishing Company of America, Baltimore, Maryland: 1992

Wagner, Ray, editor, *The Soviet Air Force in World War II: The Official History, Originally Published by the Ministry of Defense of the USSR*, Doubleday & Company, Inc., Garden City, New York: 1973

INDEX

Note: page numbers in bold refer to illustrations, captions and plates.

air formations 17, 20, 28, 30, 91
air superiority 17, 22, **55**, **70**, 76, 82, 90
air supply operations 5, **6**, 13, 14, 39–40, **40**, **42**, **46–47**, **51**, **85**, 85–90, **86**, **90**, **91**
air support for ground forces 9, 17, 20–22, 24, **63**, **86**, 91
air tactics 17, 20, 28–30, **31**, 34, 51–53, **52**, **55**, **63**, 91
air transport force **43**, 78, **78**, 87
aircraft 10, **11**, 32, 43
   Curtiss P-40 Tomahawk 32, 33
   de Havilland Mosquito **33**
   DFS 230 glider 5, 43
   Dornier Do 17 22
   Douglas A-20B Boston 33, 53, **86**
   Fiat BR20M 43, 53, 58–59, **60**
   Fieseler Storch **19**, 20, 59, 84
   Focke-Wulf Fw 189 22, 62
   Focke-Wulf Fw 200 **23**, **43**, **68**, 73, 77, 78, 79, 87, 88
   Gotha Go 242 glider 5
   Gotha Go 244 43
   Heinkel He 111 5, **5**, 9, 12, 14, 15, **15**, 22, **23**, 24, 39, **39**, 40, 41, **41**, 42, **42**, 43, **43**, 45, **46–47**, 50, 53, 54, **54**, **55**, 58, **60**, 62, 66, 67, 68, 71, 72–73, 76, 77, 78, 79, **82**, 83, 87–88
   Heinkel He 177 **23**, **43**, 73, 78, 88
   Henschel Hs 123 12, 22, 39
   Henschel Hs 129 12, 22, 39, **(63)64–65**
   Ilyushin Il-2 Shturmovik 12, 31, 32, **32**, 43, 53, 58, **58**, **60–61**, 62, 63, **63**, 77, **(79)80–81**, **85**, **86**, 87, 91
   Ilyushin Il-4 10, 32, **70**, **83**, **86**
   Junkers Ju 52 5, 14, 15, 19, 24, **24**, 34, 40, 41, **41**, 42, **42**, 43, **43**, 45, **45**, **46–47**, 49, 50, 52, **52**, 53, 54, **(55)56–57**, **60**, 66, 67, 68, 71, 72, 73, 77, 78, **78**, 79, **(79)80–81**, 82, 83, 87, 88
   Junkers Ju 86 5, 14, **23**, **39**, 43, **43**, 45, 50, 53, 58–59, **60**, 66, 67, 72, 73, 87
   Junkers Ju 87 Stuka 4, 8, **8**, 9, 9, 10, 12, **14**, **15**, 20, 22, **25**, 39, 58, **59**, 70, 73, 74, 76
   Junkers Ju 88 9, 22, 32, **33**, **60**, **66**, 67, 76
   Junkers Ju 290 **23**, **43**, **68**, 73, 87, 88
   LaGG-3 17, 31, 34, 73
   Lavochkin La-5 17, 20, 21, **26**, 31–32, **(55)56–57**
   Messerschmitt Bf 109 4, 17, **21**, 22, **25**, 28, 31, 32, 33, 39, 43, **46–47**, 49, 53, 54, **(55)56–57**, **60**, 62, **63**, **71**, 74, 76
   Messerschmitt Bf 109G "Gustav" 17, 20, **21**, 32, 79
   Messerschmitt Bf 110 Zerstörer 8, 20, **22**, **25**, 49, 54, 58, 62, 79
   MiG-3 **4**, 31
   Petlyakov Pe-2 16, 32, 33, **33**, **63**, **86**, 91
   Polikarpov I-16 20, 31
   Polikarpov I-153 20, 31
   Polikarpov R-5 reconnaissance biplane 33
   Savoia Marchetti SM.81 68
   U-2 33, **67**
   Yakovlev Yak-1 17, 20, **21**, **26**, **31**, 32, 34, **(55)56–57**
   Yakovlev Yak-7B **26**, 32
airdrop missions 16, 68, **74**, **76**, 78, 82
airfield infrastructure 18, **45**, 45–48, 68, 71, 72, **72**, **(79)80–81**, 88, **91**, 92
airfield strikes 43, 48, 53, 55, 59, 66, **66**, **(79)80–81**, **86**

ammunition supplies 40, 44, 54–55, 70, 71, 73, 86, **89**
anti-aircraft batteries **46**, **51**, 51–53, **(79)80–81**
ARMIR (Armata Italiana in Russia) 25, **25**, 59, 68
awards and medals 28

Barkhorn, Oberleutnant Gerhard 20
Battle Group Stahel 12
Budenny, Marshal Semyon **54**
bureaucratic inefficiencies 44, 49, 87

camouflage **46**, 49, **88**
Carganico, Generalmajor Victor 41, 87
cargo-carrying capacity 43, **68**, 71, 73, 88
Caucasus oilfields, the 6, 9, 10, 13
Chir line, the 25, 41, 45, 49, 54, 55, 58, 59, 63, 66, 67, 70
chronology of events 13–16
Chuikov, Gen Vasily 10
cloud and fog cover 12, 15, 46, 47, 49, 51–53, 55, **55**, 90
cold start engine procedures 78
combat attrition 17, 53, 55, 71, 83
command structures 19–20, 26, 35, 68
concentrated foods 44
conversion workshops for transport assembly 42, 78
Crimea, the 6–8, **8**, 13, 83

decision making and responsibility 35, **35**, **36**, 37–38, 87
Demyansk pocket, the 5, **6**, 13, 36, 41, 42, 92
dive-bombing techniques **8**, **46**, **60**, **63**, 70, 91
Don Front, the 4, 9, 11, **11**, 12, 14, 54, 59, 74
drop zones 82
dummy airfields **88**

evacuation of the sick and wounded, the 5, 24, 44, 73, 79, 86

Fiebig, General der Flieger Martin 8, 12, 13, 14, 16, 20, 36, 41, 48, 49, 54, 58, 66–67, 72, 82, 83, 87
field hospitals 76
fighter aces 20, 71, **84**, 91
fighter escorts 5, **46**, **47**, 48–49, 54, **(55)56–57**, 79
Fliegerverbindungsoffiziere (Luftwaffe liaison officers) 21
food rations 44, **44**, 54, 70–71, 73, 82, 86
"free hunter" (otoniki) VVS fighters **46**, 51
Freudenfeld, Major 82
fuel supplies 40, 44, 49, 54, 63, 67, 71, 73, 86, **89**
Führer Directive No. 41 13
Führer Directive No. 45 13

GAL (Grupparea Aeriana de Lupta) 25
German counteroffensive in Kharkov 84
German Heer, the
Armies
   First Panzer 83
   Fourth Panzer 12
   Sixth 4, **6**, 9, 10, 12, 14, **15**, 20, 35, **35**, 36, **36**, **37**, 40, **40**, 41, **44**, **44**, 48, **53**, 55, 63, **70**, 70–71, **71**, **74**, **75**, 76, 82, 84, 85–86, 92
   Eleventh 6, 8, 13
   Seventeenth 16, 83, 84
Army Groups
   A 6, 9, 10, 13, 15, 16, 20, 38, 39, 70, 74, 76, 83
   B 6, 9, 10, 13, 25, 77, 84
   Center 8, 13, 38
   Don 14, 16, 36, 40, 44, **53**, 59, 70, 74, 84, **86**
   North 5, 8

   South 6, 8, 13, **35**, 84
Corps
   II Corps 5
   LVII Panzer Corps 15, 55, 58, 59, **59**, **60**, 62, 63, 66, 70, 90
   X Corps 5
   XI Corps 37, 82
   XXXXVIII Panzer Corps 11, 53–54, 55
Divisions
   6th Panzer 55, 59
   7th Panzer 68
   11th Panzer 67
   17th Panzer 55, 62
   23rd Panzer 55, 59
Regiments
   99th Flak 12
German retreat to Rostov 68–70, **69**
German strategy 5–8, 9, 13, 17, 20–21, 35–38, **53**, 53–54, 55, 62, 63, 66, 67, 68, 70, **73**, 73–74, 76, 77–78, 82, 83–84
and breakout option of the Stalingrad Pocket 37, 55, 70, 86
German surrender 16, **76**, 82, 92
gliders 5, 43, 79
Göring, Hermann 35, 36, **36**, 37, **37**, 38, 41, 66, 87
ground support 4, 12, 45, 48, **48**, 50, 71, 78, 79, 83, 88–89
Gumrak Airfield **5**, 16, 48, **71**, **74**, 76, 79, 87

Hartmann, Major Erich 20
"hedgehog" defense, the **18**, 35
Hitler, Adolf 5–6, **6**, 9, 10, 12, 13, 14, 15, **19**, **35**, 35–36, 37, 37–38, 44, **53**, 55, 63, 66, 68, 70, 73, **73**, 74, 77, 79, 83, 87, 92
horse slaughtering 44, **44**, 54
Hungarian 1st Aviation Detachment (Repuloescoport), the 25
Hungarian Second Army, the 16, 25, 76–77, 85, 92

Ilyushin, Sergey 32
Italian Eighth Army, the 15, 25, 59, **61**, 62, **63**, 66, 68, **72**, 85, 90, 92
Italian Expeditionary Air Force, the **25**, 68

Jeschonnek, Generaloberst Hans 36, **36**, 37, 38
Jodl, General Alfred 37

Katte formations 17, 28, 91
Keitel, Generalfeldmarschall Wilhelm 37
Kharkov 6–8, **8**, 13, 84
Kholm airfield 5, 13
Khryukin, General-Mayor Timofey 28, **28**, 34
Kiev Front, the 28, **29**
kills and victories claimed 53, 62, **63**, 66, 74, 91
Kirov railway, the 28
Kuban Peninsula, the 83, **91**, 92
Kühl, Oberst Ernst 41, 42, 67

lend-lease program, the 33
logistical planning 18–19, 36, 40–41, 78, 85–86, 90
losses 4, 8, 9, 12, 13, 20, **30**, **38**, 39, 43, **46**, 49, 53, 54, 58, **58**, **60**, 62, **62**, 66, **66**, 67, 68, 70, 71, 72, 73, 77, 79, **79**, 84–85, 87, 88, 91
low altitude flying 4, 31, **46**, 49, 51–53, 67
Lufthansa 87
Luftwaffe, the 4, 13, **14**, 15, **17**, 17–19, **19**, 24, 26, 30, 37, 39, 42, 48–49, **49**, **61**, 71, **75**, **76**, 78, 82, **87**, 91, 92
   Air Fleets (Luftflotten) 19
      4th (Luftflotte 4) 6, 8, **8**, 10, 13, 14, 15, **16**, 18, 19–20, 22, **22**, 24, **24**, 27, 38, 39, 40, 45, 53, 58, 62, **63**, 73–74, 79, 83, 87, 90

Bomber Wings *(Kampfgeschwader)* (KG) **19**
Bomber Wing 1 (KG 1) **25**
Bomber Wing 4 (KG 4)
III./KG 4 **43**
Bomber Wing 20 (KG 20) 42
Bomber Wing 27 (KG 27) 22, 24, **25**, 83
Bomber Wing 40 (KG 40) 73
Bomber Wing 51 (KG 51) **25**, 76
Bomber Wing 55 (KG 55) 22, 24, 41, 83
Bomber Wing 76 (KG 76) **25**
Bomber Wing 100 (KG 100)
I./KG 100 **43**
Condor Legion 43
Corps *(Fliegerkorps)* 20
IV Air Corps 8, 19, 20, 58, **60**, 84
VIII Air Corps 6, **8**, 10, 12, 13, 19, 20, 21–22, 39, **40**, 41, 49, 55, 58, **60**, **68**, 72, 73, 83
Destroyer Wings *(Zerstörergeschwader)* (ZG) **19**
Destroyer Wing 1 (ZG 1) **22**, **25**, 49, 54, 58, **60–61**, 62
Divisions
9th Flak 12, 24–25, 36, 41, 48, 87
Fighter Wings *(Jagdgeschwader)* (JG) **19**, 20
Fighter Wing 3 (JG 3) 20, **25**, 41, 49, 54, 71
Fighter Wing 52 (JG 52) 20, **25**, 49
Fighter Wing 53 (JG 53) 20, 62
Fighter Wing 77 (JG 77) 20
Ground Attack Wings *(Schlachtgeschwader)* (Sch.G) **19**, 22
Ground Attack Wing 1 (Sch.G 1) **60–61**
IV./Sch.G 1 **(63)64–65**
Luftransporteinsatz Krim 83
Special Duty Bomber Wings *(Kampfgruppe zu besonderen Verwendung)* 24, **25**, 42, 43, **43**, 73
KG.z.b.V.50 24, **25**, **43**
Stuka Wings *(Stukageschwader)* (St.G) **19**, 22
Stuka Wing 1 (St.G 1) **25**, 58, **60–61**
Stuka Wing 2 (St.G 2) 41
Stuka Wing 77 (St.G 77) **25**, 58, **60–61**, 62

Maikop oilfields, the 6, 9, 13
maintenance **5**, 18, 25, 45, **48**, 78, **88**, 88–89, 90
malnutrition 54, 70, 86
Manstein, General Erich von 6, 8, 13, 15, 20, 21, **35**, 38, 50, 54, 55, 58, **60**, 62, 63, 67, 74, 83, 84
map of front lines, 1942 **7**
mechanical failures 73, 82
Milch, Generalfeldmarschall Erhard 16, 44, **73**, 77–79, 82, 87
military strength and complements 8, **11**, 27, 32, **32**, 34, 40, 42, **43**, 58, **63**, 73, 74, 78, 83, 91, 92
mission routes 49, **51**
Morozovsk airfield 14, 15, 41, 42, 45, **45**, 53, 59, **61**, 63, 67, 68, **68**, 70, 85, 88–89, 92
Morzik, Oberst Fritz 5, 41, 77, **79**, 87, 89

night missions 9, 10, 15, 28, 32, 33, **46**, 49, 55, **55**, **67**, 77, 79, 82
"Night Witches" (women pilots), the 33, **67**
North African Theater, the 35
Novikov, General-Leytenant Aleksandr 10, 14, 26–28, **27**, 30, 32, **32**, 33–34, **46**, 50–51, 55, **88**, 90, 92
Novocherkassk Airfield 15, 16, 71

Oblivskaya Airfield 12, 50
OKH *(Oberkommando des Heers)*, the 36, 37
OKW *(Oberkommando der Wehrmacht)*, the 37
Operation *Torch* (November 1942) 13, 35
operational readiness 4, 19, 20, 24, **24**, **25**, 34, 40, 48, 50, **54**, 55, 58, 71, 73, 77, 78, 83, 89–90
Operations: German
Barbarossa (June – December 1941) 13, 20, 26
Blau (June – November 1942) 6, 8, 9, 13, **18**, 20, 24, 84, 85
Donnerschlag (Thunderclap) 15, 55, 63
Fredericus (November 1942) 6, 13
Wintergewitter (Winter Storm) (December 1942) 15, 50, **54**, 55–59, **60–61**, 62, **63**, 68, 73, 86, 90, 92
Operations: Soviet Union

Koltso (Ring) (January 1943) 7**5**, 16, 74, 86
Little Saturn (December 1942) 15, 38, **58**, 59–62, **61**, 66, 68, 70, 73, 92
Uranus (November 1942) 10–12, **12**, 14, **16**, **22**, 28, 30, 32, **32**, 33, 39, 40, 45, **83**, **88**, 89, 90, 91
orders of battle **25**, **34**, **43**

para-zveno air formations 30, 34, **55**, 91
Paulus, General Friedrich 10, 11, 14, 16, **18**, 36, 37, **37**, 40, 44, 54, 63, 66, 74, **76**, 79, 85, 87
Pezzi, General Enrico 68
Pflugbeil, General Kurt 20, 58, **60**, 84
Pickert, Generalmajor Wolfgang 24, 36–37, 41, 44, 48, 76, 87
pilot experience and training 26, **28**, 30, **30**, 34, **39**, **46**, 62, 91
Pitomnik Airfield 14, 16, 39, 40, 41, 44, 48, 49, 50, 51, 66, 71, **71**, 73, 74, 76, 87
Polikarpov, Nikolai 30, 33
POWs 4, 6–8, 62, 7**7**, 85, 86
production 91–92
purges, the 26

radio homing beacons 48, 76, 79, 82
radio sets and intercepts 30, **31**, 34, **50**, 51, **55**, 91
RAF, the 22, 28
rail-line capacity 18, 40, 78, 79
Rattenkrieg 10
rear gunner positions **85**
reconnaissance 10, 12, 14, 22–24, 32, 33, 39
Red Army, the 4, 6, 16, 35, 39, 43, 66, **63**, 92
Armies 10, 28, 59, 62
2nd Guards 59, 62, 63, 68–70
5th Tank **14**, 39, 53–54, 59
51st 58, 59, **60–61**, 62, 63
Corps 28, 39
24th Tank **61**, 66, 67, 92
25th Tank 66, 67, 92
reinforcements 15, 27, 36, 62, 63, 66, 73, 91, 92
Richthofen, Generalfeldmarschall Wolfram Freiherr von 6, 8, 9, **9**, 10, **11**, 13, 14, 15, **19**, 19–20, 21–22, **35**, 36, 37, 38, 39, 40, **40**, **41**, 48, 50, 54, 58, 59, **60**, 66, 70, **73**, 74, 77, 82, 83, 84
Richthofen, Manfred von (the Red Baron) 20
Rokossovsky, Marshal Konstantin 14, 16, 54, 74, 87
Rotte formations 17, 20, 28
Rudel, Oberst Hans-Ulrich 12, **14**, 22, 39
Rudenko, General-Mayor Sergey Ignat'yevich 50–51
Rumanian Army, the 12, **79**
Armies
Fourth Army 10, **12**, 25, 85
Third Army 10, 11, **12**, 14, 25, 85
Corps 55, 70
Russo-Finnish War, the 26, 28

Salsk Airfield 15, 16, 66, 68, 70, 71, **71**, 72, 77, **79**, 90, 92
Schede, Major Kurt 73
Schentke, Lt Georg 71
Schmidt, General Arthur 37, 66
serviceability rates 18, 42, 43, 77
Sevastopol 6, 8, **8**, 13, 18, 20, 21, 58
Seydlitz-Kurzbach, General Walther von 37
shortages 18, 25, 37, **48**, 53, 54, 59, 79, 82, **83**, 88
Smirnov, General-Mayor Konstantin 77
sortie rates 14, **42**, 45, 62, 63, 68, 71, 74, 76, 77, 84, 85, 87, 88, **90**, 92
sourcing and conversion of planes for air transport 87
Southwest Front, the 14
Soviet air blockade, the **46**, **47**, 50–53, **52**, 55, **(55)56–57**, 58, 66, 74, **84**, 92
Soviet intercepts **(55)56–57**
Soviet strategy 5, 8–9, 10, **11**, 13, **18**, 20, 30, 38, **38**, 50–51, 59, 62, 66, 67, 74, 76–77, **86**, **88**, 90–91, 92
Spanish Civil War, the 20, **39**, 43
spare parts 45, 59
SS, the
II Panzer Corps 73
Wiking Division 68

Stahel, Col Reiner 12
Stalin, Joseph 9–10, 13, 26, 30, 33, 35, 38, **38**, **54**, 59, 62, 67
Stalingrad **9**, 9–10, 35
Stalingrad Air Defense (PVO) Corps 51
Stalingrad Front, the 4, 12, 14
Stalingrad pocket, the **5**, 12, **18**, 51, 76, **76**
Stalino airfield 45, 73
Stavka (Soviet High Command) 5, 9, **11**, 12, 13, 27, 28, 34, 74, 90, 92
Strecker, General Kurt 82
supplies delivered 5, 13, 14, 40, 50, 53, 54–55, **60**, 66, 68, 70, 73, 79, 82, 85, **85**, **90**
supply containers 36, 78, 82, **89**
supply lines 4, 8, 9, 10, 13, 18, 24, 28, 40, 78, 86
supply quality 44
supply requirements 5, 36, 38, 40, 44, 50, 54, 63, 66, 70, 73, 85–86

Taganrog airfield 76, **77**, 78, 87
tanks 53, 54, **62**, **(63)64–65**, **66**, 68, 85
Tatsinskaya Airfield 15, 40, 41, 43, 45, **45**, 50, 53, 59, **61**, **62**, 63, **66**, 66–67, 68, **68**, 70, 85, 88–89
Third Battle of Kharkov, the 16
transport capabilities and ranges **23**, 24, 71, 72, 73
transport plane assembly 42–43, **43**, 78, **78**, 87

unit structures and organization 17, **17**, **19**, 19–20, 26–27, 28, **29**, 84
unloading and distribution 48
urban warfare 10, **11**, 13

Valentik, Major Dmitriy 70
Vasilevsky, Colonel-General Aleksandr **38**, **54**, 59
Vatutin, Lt Gen Nikolai 14
Voronezh Front, the 76–77
Voronezh-Kharkov offensive, the 16
Voronov, Marshal Nikolay 14
VVS (Soviet Air Force), the 4, 4, 5, 8, 9, 10, 12, **12**, 13, 14, **16**, 17, 18, 26–27, **27**, 30, **30**, 38, 40, **46**, 49, **50**, **54**, **58**, 72, 74, 77, **(79)80–81**, 83, **84**, **85**, **86**, 90–91, 92
ADD (Long-Range Aviation) 10, **11**, 28, 32, 51, **70**, 76, 82, 90
Air Armies (VA) 27, 28, **33**
2nd VA 27, 77
8th VA 9, 10, 27, 28, **28**, **29**, 31, 32, 33, **34**, 51, 58, 62–63, 66, 74, 90
16th VA 10, 12, 27, 34, **34**, 50, 51, 58, 62–63, 66, 71, 74, 82, 90
17th VA 10, 12, 27, **34**, 51, 59–62, 74, 90
Divisions 28, 53
102nd Air Defense (PVO) 51, 90
Regiments 53, 70
3rd Guards Fighter **(55)56–57**
9th Guards Independent Fighter 34, **(55)56–57**, 59, 62, 91

Warmewagen (warming) vehicles 48, 66, 72, 78, 88
weaponry 32, **46**, 51, 66, 72
37mm anti-aircraft gun (USSR) **51**
MK 101 anti-tank cannon (Germany) 62, **(63)64–65**
weather conditions 4, 12, 14, 18, 39, **45**, 48, **48**, 50, 53, 55, 59, 66, 67, 71, 72, 77, **77**, 79, 82, **82**, 83, **83**, 87, 88, 89, 90
Weidinger, General Dr.-Ing Hanns 77

Yeremenko, General Andrey 12, 14
Yeremin, Major **84**

Zeitzler, General Kurt 36, 37, 70
Zhigarev, General Pavel 26
Zhukov, General Georgi **38**
Zverevo airfield 16, 72, **72**, 77, **(79)80–81**, 89, 92